D0552317

The Arts in Your Church

A practical guide

The Arts in Your Church

A practical guide

Fiona Bond

Copyright © 2001 Fiona Bond
This edition copyright © 2001 Piquant
The moral rights of the author and illustrators have been asserted.

First edition 2001

06 05 04 03 02 01 7 6 5 4 3 2 1

ISBN 1–903689–00–7

Published by Piquant
PO Box 83, Carlisle, CA3 9GR, United Kingdom
E-mail: info@piquant.net
Website: www.piquant.net

All Rights Reserved.

Permission to use any material from this book for professional or commercial
purposes should be made to the author through Piquant.

A Catalogue Record of this book is available in the UK from the British Library.

Cover design: Pool 31
Typeset by Saxon Graphics Ltd, Derby
Printed in Singapore

Contents

Foreword

It is rare to find a book that really does fill a gap, but in this case, you are holding one which simply has no parallels. It is unique in a number of important ways.

First, it combines vision with practical advice. There are many books which paint a stirring picture of the arts in the purposes of God, and a number which will tell you how to set up successful Christian art projects – but none which link the two so clearly and show you how to turn the vision into a practical reality.

Second, the book shows that the church cannot afford to treat the arts as mere illustrations, to be left behind once 'the point' has been clearly grasped by the mind. The arts do their own kind of work in their own kind of way, helping people dig deep to unlock Christian truth, with breathtaking power to touch head and heart. The arts are indispensable for the church, and especially in a culture like ours which is increasingly alert and alive to all things artistic and aesthetic. *The Arts in Your Church* shows us how to demonstrate this in very practical ways.

Third, the author's background and professional life make her uniquely qualified to write a book like this. As well as being a practising musician and trained in theology, Fiona Bond has extensive professional expertise in arts management, setting up numerous arts events, not only in churches but in many secular settings. This remarkable range of experience and gifts informs the pages which follow. Here is an author who lives and breathes what she writes.

For two years, it was my pleasure and privilege to have Fiona as my colleague and Project Manager in the 'Theology Through the Arts' project at the University of Cambridge. 'Theology Through the Arts' is designed to show how different forms of art can help us explore the riches of the Christian faith. Setting it up was a risky venture, but the fact that it is now firmly established and has led to so many other things is due in no small part to Fiona's ability to inspire others, and to convince people they can do much more than they imagine. This has had its mark on the book. It is not only a first-rate guide for those who have already decided to run arts events or commission church art – it will also inspire those who have never thought of doing either to move swiftly into action. Fiona shows we really have nothing to be afraid of and everything to gain.

Jeremy Begbie
Cambridge, UK

Preface

This book takes a very practical approach to a very practical need. From 1997–99, I was involved in setting up a project at Cambridge University, UK, under the direction of Dr Jeremy Begbie, titled 'Theology Through the Arts'. By bringing together a mixture of top Christian thinkers and top artists from a range of disciplines, exciting methods of working together were developed in order to breathe new life into the academic discipline of theology. The project grew at an unbelievable rate. It was very soon apparent that academic theology was just one of many arenas in which Christians were hungry to engage with the arts in new ways. Within weeks of the launch of 'Theology Through the Arts', the office was inundated with calls from church leaders and artists from all over the world. Some gave inspiring accounts of successful projects already undertaken; this was welcome encouragement for the new project. The vast majority of calls, though, were from people who were excited by the idea of exploring faith through different art forms and who believed that they were being called by God into this direction. What they most needed was some practical help to get started.

That's where this book comes in. It certainly isn't a comprehensive account of the relationship between the arts and the church. Nor does it offer a critique of the historical role of art in churches or an analysis of the role of the arts in a multi-media age. These topics are all covered more thoroughly by other people in books better suited to that task. I have listed some of these in the Resource Section at the back.

Instead, this book is designed to be a user-friendly and practical guide for Christians who would like to deepen their knowledge of the Creator through creative means. The possibilities are so vast that sometimes it is helpful to have a starting point. I hope this book might help people to locate that starting point and give them some pointers as to how to proceed from there.

During my work with 'Theology Through the Arts', I have been privileged to come across many inspiring examples of how the arts can enrich the faith and life of individuals and church communities. Sometimes a real-life example can be more helpful than a list of guidelines. If a picture paints a thousand words, then surely a good case study could give chapters' worth of valuable insight; so I have punctuated this book with the voices of many different people who have found value in the church-arts interface. These examples are not designed to be either prescriptive or comprehensive. There are many excellent projects not mentioned in these pages. I have tried to choose examples from different sized projects in different kinds of communities whose principles could be transferred to work well in many different contexts. These examples range from a pastor who has discovered the pastoral potential of poetry to a church that employs a full-time young composer as part of its ministry to a student population.

These projects are the tip of the iceberg. Exciting and enriching things can happen when churches have the courage, and the discipline, to engage with the arts. In a world that speaks through images and music as well as words, it will be increasingly important that churches explore and articulate their faith through the arts. I hope that this book might help to make that process a little less daunting and even more rewarding.

There are many people who have influenced this book in many ways and to whom I am very grateful. Among these, I would like to make special mention of the authors of the Case Studies for their willingness to share an exciting range of experiences. My particular thanks go to the Begbie family for all their encouragement, to Peter Cousins, Pieter and Elria Kwant for their good-humoured patience through the editing process and to my family – especially my husband Bruce Longenecker – for being supportive in every way imaginable.

Fiona Bond

Illustrations

Case study 1. Jeremy Begbie leads a workshop at St Edmundsbury Cathedral, Suffolk. 'Hearing is Believing', 14 November 1998. Photograph copyright Pam Pitts. Used with permission.

Case study 2. A festival offers opportunities for everyone to get involved: Tent Event, Exeter, 1987. Photograph copyright Sarah Derrick. Used with permission.

Case study 3. Katherine Freeze conducts one of her compositions at UPC, Seattle, October 2000. Photograph copyright UPC of Seattle (Washington).Used with the permission of Katherine Freeze.

Case study 4. Bobby Baker: 'The Woman who Mistook Her Mouth for a Pocket', A performance at St Luke's Church, Islington (London) as part of the 'Art in Sacred Spaces' project, May 2000. Photograph by Andrew Whittuck. Used with permission.

Case study 5. One of Australia's premiere jazz ensembles 'Clarion Fracture Zone' performs 'Canticle', a work commissioned by the Paddington Uniting Church based on the biblical love poem *Song of Songs*. This work is now available on CD recording, 1999.

Case study 6. 'Defying Dog' by David Cotterrell, an interactive video piece, exploring the changing role of churches in a multimedia age, commissioned for 'Art in Sacred Spaces' and installed at The Round Church, Hackney, London, May 2000. Copyright David Cotterrell. Used with permission.

Case study 7. A warm-up session for a group of teenagers, 'Inside out' project, Kettle's Yard, Cambridge, 1990. Photograph copyright Sarah Derrick. Used with permission.

Case study 8. A creative writing session fires imagination as part of David Cotterrell's work at Rushmore Primary School in Clapton, Hackney for 'Art in Sacred Spaces', May 2000. Copyright David Cotterrell. Used with Permission.

Case study 9. Dress rehearsal for 'The Depostion' with dancers from Icon Dance company, September 2000. Copyright Sara Savage. Used with permission.

Case study 10. *Cyberspace*, a digital image. Copyright Jonathan Kearney. Used with permission.

Section 1. Bobby Baker: 'The Woman who Mistook Her Mouth for a Pocket', A performance at St Luke's Church, Islington (London) as part of the 'Art in Sacred Spaces' project, May 2000. Photograph by Andrew Whittuck. Used with permission.

Section 2. Constructing set and staging needs hard work and patience. Copyright Jeremy Begbie, TTA. Used with permission.

Section 3. A 'hands-on' exploration of sculpture with work by Ernesto Neto, 2000. Copyright DCA. Photograph by Sarah Derrick. Used with permission.

Section 4. Children's painting workshop led by Ian Davenport, at Dundee Contemporary Arts, 1999. Copyright DCA. Used with permission.

Cartoons copyright Charlie Mackesy. Used with permission.

Section 1

Arts, Church and Artists

Section 1. Bobby Baker: 'The Woman who Mistook Her Mouth for a Pocket', A performance at St Luke's Church, Islington (London) as part of the 'Art in Sacred Spaces' project, May 2000 (photo: Andrew Whittuck).

"Could we have that last one again?"

1

The Arts in Contemporary Culture

We live in exciting times! There cannot be many places left in the industrialized world where developments in technology have not profoundly changed the way that we access, handle and communicate information. Many billions of pounds are spent each year on image-based advertising in the belief that it can communicate a sophisticated range of information in just a few seconds. The average person in the West spends over 1500 hours per year in front of the television or video screen (almost as many hours as a full-time job), soaking up a breathtaking range of visual, musical and verbal information. As a culture, we believe that the visual / aural / verbal realm of communication has such power to influence belief and behaviour that an entirely new industry is springing up to safeguard us and our children from TV shows, computer games, videos, movies and web content that might be damaging. [See Case Study 10]▶

In this environment, it is hardly surprising that our culture is becoming increasingly sensitive to visual, musical and other artistic stimuli. Even people who would not describe themselves as 'artistic' often spend time and money on communicating something about themselves, their values and aspirations, through their home, garden, clothes, hair, choice of music, way of speaking and other aesthetic features of life.

These aspects of life don't always qualify as 'art', but they can be seen as evidence of a wider phenomenon. In contemporary western culture, we are used to receiving information and thinking about issues through a combination of visual, musical and verbal stimuli. We acknowledge the power of the multi-media message by spending time and money to ensure that the sounds and images we display to other people about ourselves correspond to what we choose to convey.

As Christians, we may want to take issue with a culture driven by the values of consumerism but, regardless of the underlying values of the multi-media revolution, it has changed the way we deal with images, music and words. You could say that these combined media have, in some ways, become the 'language' of our time.

To demonstrate the point: in 1828 the primary Webster's Dictionary definition of 'language' was focused on verbal communication: '*Human speech; the expression of ideas by words or significant articulate sounds, for the communication of thoughts.*'[1] By the twentieth century, the primary definition had changed to accommodate a broader understanding of language: '*Any means of conveying or communicating ideas; specifically, human speech.*'[2]

If the definition of language is changing, perhaps that points to a change in the nature of language. There is no longer the assumption that language is about verbal communication alone. The multi-media communications industry makes its millions on the assumption that image, sound and word combine to communicate in a way that is greater than the sum of the parts.[3]

While the popular media revolution ensures that visual, musical and verbal messages are generated and understood in increasingly subtle ways, old divisions between 'highbrow' and 'popular' arts are being broken down and art is becoming an increasingly interesting political issue.

In recent research carried out by MORI in the UK (commissioned by the Arts Council of England), 95 per cent of people interviewed believed that children should have more experience of the arts at school than they currently receive. This is reinforced by further MORI statistics showing that the arts are considered important to the economic and cultural health of society and that people believe their lives are richer for experiencing the arts.[4]

In his New Statesman Arts Lecture 2000, Gerry Robinson, Chairman of the Arts Council of England, states:

> The arts can no longer be characterized as a middle- or upper-class pursuit. Research shows that, even in the lower income groups, half of all adults participate in the arts: that's more than the number who participate in sport.[5]

---

1   *Webster's Dictionary*, 1828.
2   *Webster's Dictionary*, Revised and Unabridged, 1913.
3   Cf. Jeremy Begbie, 'Prayer and Music', in *Perspectives on Prayer*, ed. Fraser Watts, (London: SPCK, 2001), 70.
4   Gerry Robinson, *The Creativity Imperative: Investing in the Arts in the 21st Century* (London: Arts Council of England, 2000), 2.
5   Ibid., 2.

For the first time in decades, there is a new will among politicians to put money into the arts. A number of recent high-profile arts initiatives in the UK have demonstrated that far from offering cultural 'icing on the cake', the arts have a unique ability to catalyse a local or regional economy. When Glasgow was made European City of Culture in 1990, the initiative was ridiculed by the media. Few people realized how the city would be transformed for the better by the money levied on this cultural ticket. In a remarkably short space of time, the city has established a new economic base centred on the creative service sector, and has risen from a period of industrial decline to become one of Europe's most vibrant and creatively active cities. Many other cities have followed suit with equal success and the arts are firmly on the political agenda as an agent for economic development. John Steele (Group Personnel Director for BT) writes:

> The arts have immense power to add to the quality of all our lives…
> But this is not just about brightening people's lives; the arts constitute
> a particularly vibrant part of our national economy … providing jobs
> and acting as a motor for local regeneration.[6]

One of the reasons that the arts have become an agent for economic development is that they were already recognized for their potential to affect social change by challenging attitudes (for example, to race, class, gender or disability) and helping people to learn new patterns of thought and behaviour. The very factors that alarm us about the potential for the arts to corrupt behaviour have been harnessed for good in social work, psychotherapy, education and rehabilitation. [See Case Study 5]▶

At a wider level, the arts and popular culture can stimulate social change by giving voice to individuals and groups who do not hold political or economic power. In a private consultation paper for 'Theology Through the Arts', John de Gruchy of the University of Capetown writes:

> The struggle against apartheid produced an artistic creativity of
> remarkable intensity and there can be little doubt that the arts were
> significant within the broader struggle. Nadine Gordimer, the cele-
> brated South African novelist rightly noted that 'art is at the heart
> of liberation'.[7]

---

6   John Steele (Group Personnel Director for BT), Introduction in *Re-creating Communities: Business, The Arts and Regeneration* (ed. Phyllida Shaw; London: Arts & Business, 1999), inside flap.

7   John de Gruchy, citing Nadine Gordimer, *Culture in Another South Africa* (ed. William Campschreur & Joost Divendal; London: Zed Books, 1989), 12.

The arts have also become a valuable resource for industry. Success in the marketplace often depends on a company's ability to think and act creatively. An increasing number of companies have taken to modelling their creative processes through 'arts-based training' in order to exercise and refine those skills in their employees. In describing why a training course run by Trestle Theatre Company worked so well, Karen Crowshaw of the Halifax Bank said:

> Actors think differently from the way we do – they take you out of your tunnel vision. And the irony is, it's such good value compared with sending people on outside courses. It's the only course I can recall that people consistently talk about and remember.[8]

So what does all this mean for Christians? The Reformation in the sixteenth century was motivated largely by a recognition that the Christian message was no longer reaching people in a language they understood and that this had become a stumbling block for the individual faith of ordinary people. While a similar challenge could be said to face churches today, the irony is that the Reformers' mission laid some of the foundations for a relationship between (particularly Reformed Protestant) churches and the arts that has proved rocky to say the least.

Surely there is a huge opportunity at stake. If the arts are playing an enhanced role in western culture and if new technology is ensuring that we engage with ideas through a combination of visual, musical and verbal media, then it would make sense for Christians to embrace the arts with enthusiasm. But change and challenge of any kind often provoke fear and opposition. In engaging with the arts from a Christian perspective, it can be wise to learn from some of the problems that have faced Christians and artists in their work together.

---

8   Karen Crowshaw of the Halifax Bank, talking about training with Trestle Theatre Company, in *It Worked For Them* (London: Arts & Business, 2000), 11.

2

The Arts in the Church

2.1 A rocky relationship

Of course, there is already a wonderful tradition of articulating the Christian faith through visual art, music and even drama, dance and film. Sixty per cent of the average church service involves music of some kind, and there are few church buildings that are not decorated by sculpture, stained glass, paintings, banners or other visual reminders of the Christian faith. Church architecture itself can be a powerful reminder of the foundation and shape of the faith it describes. **[See Case Study 5]▶**
Looking further back to the roots of Christianity, the Bible is rich with different uses of the written and spoken word. Its meaning is enlivened through poetry, drama, storytelling and song lyric. Its pages tell of music, dance, drama, architecture and visual art undertaken throughout history as a means of glorifying God. Jesus himself grew up in a family of artisans and was known as a carpenter by those in his home town (Mark 6: 3). We get telling glimpses into his creative flair through the subtle play of imagery and message in his narrative parables.[9] **[See Case Study 4]▶**

Despite rich historical links between the Christian faith and the creative arts, a mutual suspicion often sours the relationship on both sides. There are many reasons why the world of professional, contemporary art is sometimes seen as problematic (perhaps even inappropriate) in a church environment. Different Christian denominations have different historical

---

9   Recent work on Jesus' parables recognizes them to be 'first order artistry', in other
    words, the kind of creative endeavour that can affect worldviews, as opposed to
    'second order artistry' that is simply illustrative in intention and effect. Cf B.W.
    Longenecker in an unpublished paper for 'Theology Through the Arts' consultation,
    September 2000.

sensitivities when it comes to artistic expression. While this book cannot hope to offer a detailed critique of these, some have become such an intrinsic part of wider Christian and artistic attitudes that it is worth mentioning them.

Like any powerful means of expressing ideas, creativity can be used and abused, and this may lie at the heart of much Christian suspicion towards the arts. The sad irony of the third commandment – which was being broken almost as it was being given – lies heavily.

> You shall not make for yourself an idol in the form of anything in heaven above or in the earth beneath or in the waters below. You shall not bow down to them or worship them; for I the Lord your God am a jealous God (*Exodus 20: 4*).

It is easy to point out that the average sculptor or composer has absolutely no intention of turning her latest work into a shrine, and that we're not nearly as susceptible to worshipping graven images as our Old Testament forebears. Yet we already know that almost any human pleasure can slip from healthy engagement to all-consuming passion, and the arts are no exception. If we acknowledge a special place in culture for the arts, then we perhaps acknowledge a special danger too. Both the Guggenheim in Bilbao and the Tate Modern gallery in London have been hailed as cathedrals to modern art. The architecture of movie theatres is often an unashamed pastiche on the temples of antiquity, while a recent survey revealed that more young people associate religious experience with going to a movie rather than going to church. German artist Gerhard Richter goes so far as to say; 'Art is not a substitute for religion: it is a religion. The church is no longer adequate as a means of affording experience of the transcendental.'[10]

Much of the artistic revelling of our culture does smack of idolatry. Image is everything and, in the struggle to be 'in the world but not of it', it is easy, and tempting, to overstep the mark on the side of idolatry. Yet, as Jeremy Begbie points out:

> No theology will ever be free of the risk of idolatry, since it is always mediated through creaturely thought-forms, activities and so on. The critical question to ask is: what does the risk yield? All good theology

---

10   Quoted in Makoto Fujimura, "River Grace", *Image: A Journal of the Arts*, No. 22 (1999), 32.

is done on the cliff-edge – one step too far and you tumble into idolatry, one step back and the view is never so good.[11]

Another cause for Christian hesitation over engagement with the arts is that throughout history, many artistic movements and activities have been associated with lifestyles and practices that Christians were trying to discourage. Some of the Christian Fathers advised against the practice of drama – not because drama was a problem *per se* but because it had become a 'licentious representation of decadent paganism'.[12] Yet when the dominant culture had become Christian, drama became important in the medieval church as a means of teaching a largely illiterate population about the Christian faith.

Likewise, the Reformers of the sixteenth century have been accused of throwing the artistic baby out with the bath water. When Calvin says, 'Whatever men learn of God in images is futile, indeed false',[13] it is hard to draw any other conclusion. Yet it is also Calvin who acknowledges that

> The invention of the arts, and other things which serve the common use and convenience of life, is a gift of God by no means to be despised, and a faculty worthy of commendation.[14]

No doubt the Reformers were torn. Whatever their personal preferences (and both Luther and Calvin reveal a healthy aesthetic appreciation),[15] the arts in general represented much of what they opposed. Until people were able to read Scripture directly and take the path of 'faith alone', everything else was seen as a distraction to salvation.

The legacy of this approach has been surprisingly persistent in much of the Reformed tradition, fuelled from time to time by the excesses of the artistic world. It is never quite expressed in this way but there appears to be an underlying fear that the arts inherently encourage indulgence, lack of self-control and ultimately corruption both in the lives of artists and the content of their work. On the other hand, anyone who has watched a dancer, musician, actor or artist in training knows that exceptional dedication, commitment and self-discipline are required from the majority of serious artists, with no guarantee of financial reward or popular success.

---

11   Jeremy Begbie, *Theology, Music and Time* (Cambridge: Cambridge University Press, 2000), 279.
12   Hilary Brand and Adrienne Chaplin, *Art and Soul* (Carlisle: Solway, 1999), 26.
13   Calvin, Institutes 1.11.5.
14   Calvin, *Commentary on Genesis* (chapter 4, verse 20).
15   See Brand and Chaplin, *Art and Soul*, 29–34.

With regard to artistic content, William Dyrness points out that we should not be surprised if the arts

> often express values that are at odds with a Christian view of life. In fact one is tempted to say that until Christians and the church get serious about supporting the arts, as they have done in the past, they ought to temper their criticism of the kind of art that is produced. Meanwhile if they are serious about their involvement in culture, they should take seriously their role as patrons of the arts.[16]

While Christians wrestle with mixed attitudes to the arts, there is suspicion and fear from the other side too. Much twentieth-century art was driven by a belief that visual art, in particular, was limited by a history of religious patronage, and that art independent of a church perspective demonstrates greater integrity. Most contemporary artists, of all disciplines, would now acknowledge that it is virtually impossible to create art in a cultural and religious vacuum. Art is bound to reflect the values and background of its human creators. Nonetheless, nervousness remains that the motives of some churches in embarking on an artistic project can constrict and devalue the creative process, compromising quality.

Nervousness about the quality of the contemporary arts in churches is a sensitive issue. Many of us will have squirmed in our seats through church performances which fall short not only of the glory of God but also of the junior school production down the road and last month's amateur dramatic production in the town hall. Judging the quality of art is often a subjective response influenced by taste and personal preference. As a general principle, though, the success of art in churches is not always directly proportional to talent and budget. It is influenced by vision, commitment, integrity, good planning and a willingness to offer our best to God. Motivation, commitment, sincerity, determination, personal responsibility, unselfishness and hard work are the qualities that touch even hardened art critics when they assess work of distinction. These are also some of the qualities that we are exhorted to embrace as Christians.

Despite a rocky relationship between arts and the church, an increasing number of main-stream artists are discovering a new interest in the Christian faith. An increasing number of churches are discovering that art can explore difficult issues with subtlety and wit. It can help to clarify

---

16 William Dyrness, *Visual Faith: Art, Theology and Worship* (forthcoming, Baker, 2001), 9 in author's manuscript.

perception and illuminate belief. It can offer working models for the relationship between individual and community. It can revitalize worship. It can bring us closer to the creator God in whose image we are made.

2.2. Art as a foreign language

While it may be possible to recognize and rise above many of the issues that have affected the historical church-arts relationship, there is a much more basic hurdle facing churches that want to engage with the contemporary arts. A great deal of contemporary artistic practice (regardless of discipline) is, quite frankly, bewildering to anyone who is not familiar with its historical, political, social or ideological context. From black squares on a black background, to dance in which the performers stand still, there is plenty in recent art history to generate frustration. The idea of faith engaging with contemporary arts may not be greeted with enthusiasm by those who feel they just don't 'get' contemporary art.

Even art critics are begging for mercy from an art world that is less intent on shifting the goal posts than on changing the rules or even dispensing with them completely. How can art be evaluated when there are no rules?

Art critic, Matthew Collings, took a wry look at the London arts world in *A Day in the Life of British Art*, published in *The Observer* in March 2000. Describing a conversation with a gallery owner, he admits to looking as if he understands what's going on, even when he doesn't:

> I nod and frown and absolutely agree, inwardly wondering what we're talking about while outwardly keeping the stylish leaning and swaying and gesturing going, for the benefit of Tony, the *Observer*'s photographer, who is clicking away, revving us up to great feats of intellectual posing.[17]

Exasperated with what he sees as a lack of quality control in contemporary art, critic Brian Sewell declares: 'If all this is art, I know no word that can fit the work of Michelangelo and Titian.'[18] Hans Rookmaaker, a former Professor of Art History at the Free University of Amsterdam, pointed out:

---

17 Matthew Collings, 'A Day in the Life of British Art', (*The Observer*, London, 19 March 2000).
18 Brian Sewell, *An Alphabet of Villains* (London: Bloomsbury, 1995), 27.

> The fact that so many books are published that deal with the arts is not a proof that people are sure what art is about, rather the opposite. This quest for meaning in the arts is a sign of crisis in the arts.[19]

If even the critics are confused about what art is, what it should do and how it should be evaluated, what hope does the average church have?

The up-side of all this confusion is that, in an arts world without boundaries, the church is in as good a position as anyone else to engage with the arts in new and exciting ways. In many places it is doing just that. **[See Case Study 6]▶**

While the quest to define the boundaries of art will probably go on testing the limits of our sensibilities, a climate in which 'anything goes' legitimizes a kind of artistic democracy and liberates creativity in many exciting directions. For example:

> Experiment with improvization in theatre, dance, music and even film has led to a realization that the *process* of creativity can be as valuable as the product. This has produced all kinds of spin-offs for the role of the arts in education and therapy.
>
> New respect for traditional ethnic arts has opened the door to fresh influences and new dialogue between cultures.
>
> The blurring of boundaries between 'highbrow' arts and popular culture has broken down many cultural and economic barriers to participation, making it easier for ordinary people to benefit from public art programmes.

Some of the results of artistic experimentation may be difficult to engage with at first. They are not necessarily easy on the ear, eye or brain; but then even when reading the Bible or listening to a sermon, it's sometimes the difficult bits that have the most significant impact. A friend with no training in the arts recently described this better than anyone else I've heard:

> There was this piece of art that was just a white canvas and it was titled 'canvas'. I didn't get it at all and it really annoyed me. It annoyed me so much that it forced me to think about what it might mean and why. A year later and it's the only piece I remember from the exhibition.[20]

---

19 Hans Rookmaaker, *Art Needs No Justification* (Leicester: IVP, 1978), Chapter 1.
20 Jo Robinson, in conversation.

The great thing about art is that it is good at stimulating enquiry without demanding easy answers. Like learning a new language, art invites us to think differently about familiar things. Learning the Inuit words that we call 'snow' or the Greek words that we translate 'love' implies an enhanced understanding of 'snow' or 'love' that our language is not so equipped to describe. A new vocabulary can be liberating – even if it takes some time and effort to understand it.[21]

2.3 Art as a new vocabulary

Just as the Christian faith is about 'heart' as well as 'head', action as well as thought, so the arts are about process as well as product. Sometimes the exercise of exploring an idea or a text through a creative process can itself bring new insight. For example, in Henri Nouwen's book, *The Return of the Prodigal Son*,[22] Jesus' parable (*Luke 15: 11–32*) undergoes creative engagement first from Rembrandt (in his painting of the same name) and then from Nouwen, as he reflects on both the original parable and Rembrandt's painting. The story is re-examined through two different media and two different perspectives. Different elements of the original story are highlighted, bringing new insight into God's relation to us as both Creator and Father.

So what can the arts do in and for the church? The list is potentially as boundless as the imagination. From raising issues with young people by watching a movie to the Two Cathedrals Festival in Derry that seeks to mend divided communities of Catholics and Protestants through music; from rediscovering the Bible through the art of storytelling to exploring prayer through Indian dance. In undertakings like these, there are a number of common threads. The arts have the capacity to:

– Make people think differently

There is little doubt that good art has an amazing capacity to show familiar things in unfamiliar ways. There is less agreement as to how this happens. Perhaps the arts let us experience the world from someone else's perspective or perhaps they encourage us to think with different parts of the brain. Describing the power of film, a movie-maker at a recent conference I attended

---

21 From conversations with Jeremy Begbie.
22 Henri J. M. Nouwen, *The Return of the Prodigal Son: A Story of Homecoming* (London: Darton, Longman & Todd, 1992).

said that it is only by taking people to the heart of their worldview that they can be challenged to change it. **[See Case Studies 8 and 4]▶**

– Do theology

The arts, as legitimate ways of thinking, surely have a contribution to make to Christian theology. Frank Burch Brown, an advisor to 'Theology Through the Arts', explains why:

> Supposing theology to be something like 'faith in search of under-standing' (cf. Anselm and Augustine), we can say that the arts are theologically significant insofar as they deepen the understandings important to Christian faith. These are insights into self, others, and world in relation to God – especially (for Christians) to the story and person of Christ.[23]

[See Case Study 1]▶

– Stimulate people to think about and take responsibility for their faith

Many church members feel ill-equipped to give a verbal justification for their views on a particular issue. If verbal reasoning is the only means by which faith can be acceptably articulated, there is a tendency for some people to become 'observer' Christians, not taking true responsibility for thinking about the wider implications of their faith. This can mean never taking the lead on matters of principle or (perhaps worse) taking a lead informed by hand-me-down theology that has lost its grace and subtlety in the process. The arts can offer a route by which issues arising from faith can be explored and articulated in ways that are more natural to some people. **[See Case Study 2]▶**

– Build community

There are some art forms (for example, drama, dance, film-making and music) that by their nature demand trust, co-operation and co-dependence. Achievement depends on the commitment and disciplined ability of more than one person. The church, with its commitment to 'one body, many

---

23 Frank Burch Brown, in an unpublished paper for 'Theology Through the Arts', September 2000.

parts,' could model and even develop true community through the creative process. [See Case Study 5]▶

– Challenge social assumptions and change behaviour

By encouraging people to think differently, the arts have the ability to challenge and change assumptions and behaviour. This is one of the reasons that the arts now have a major role in therapy and rehabilitation. It is easy to pay lip service to acceptable attitudes about race, gender or power structures, but it is much harder to change destructive patterns of behaviour. A film like *My Name is Joe*, a book like *I Know Why the Caged Bird Sings*, or role-play among young offenders, are a few examples of how the arts demonstrate consequences, model contrasting patterns of behaviour and enable people to encounter the world through the eyes and ears of someone else. [See Case Studies 5 and 7]▶

– Build skills and help people to live as God intended

Ninety-five per cent of people in the UK believe that children should have more experience of the arts at school.[24] This is, at least in part, because when we learn to act, dance, write poems and stories, play a musical instrument or draw a picture, we learn a variety of skills that are transferable, valuable and enjoyable. By engaging both head and heart, the arts allow us to discover that we have been 'fearfully and wonderfully made'(*Psalm 139: 14*). By using our creativity, we tap into something fundamental about being made in the image of our creator. [See Case Studies 3 and 9]▶

– Enhance ministry

Because the arts deal with the stuff of our lives, they are ideally placed to address issues of ministry. CS Lewis's account of the death of his wife, Joyce Gresham, has touched millions of people struggling with the 'why' of bereavement through the book, play and film versions of *Shadowlands*. Sometimes doing something creative with anger, fear or rage can be therapeutic. Sometimes truth can be told less destructively through metaphor. Sometimes bad decisions can be avoided by role-playing their consequences. [See Case Study 8]▶

---

24 Gerry Robinson, (see Note 4 above), 2.

– Enhance worship

'Let them praise his name with dancing and make music to him with tambourine and harp. For the Lord takes delight in his people; he crowns the humble with salvation. Let the saints rejoice in this honour and sing for joy on their beds' *(Psalm 149: 3–5).*

The role of the arts in worship has always been an important part of the Judaeo-Christian tradition, although style and form have varied, of course. As creative expression plays an enhanced role in our wider culture, I believe that churches are being called to 'sing to the Lord a new song' in the language of our time with all the risk, hard work, passion, truth and joy that entails. [See examples in all Case Studies]▶

3

The Church
and the Artist

The Artist

3.1 Respect and responsibility

A new renaissance in the church's engagement with the arts is ensuring that there are many exciting and inspiring things happening all over the world. Yet many artists remain wary of getting too involved with churches. The secular arts world is renewing its interest in what could loosely be described as 'spirituality', but it has tended to shy away from engaging with organized religion. The fact is that contemporary art (of all disciplines) in churches has sometimes had a dubious reputation. There are a number of reasons for this, and it is worth considering some of the factors that might limit potentially fruitful relationships between churches and artists.

When the arts are seen simply as a tool or instrument for illustrating theology, politics or any other ideology, then the artist becomes little more than an agent of propaganda. No matter how worthy the point being made, art treated primarily as an instrument for something else will be of limited artistic merit. The creative process is limited by pre-defining the product, and no artist wants to be accused of producing propaganda rather than art.

While most churches would share a distaste for propaganda, it is really common to see art in churches limited to purely illustrative functions. This amounts to a kind of settling for 'second best' that allows art to reinforce or embellish theology but doesn't give it permission to challenge or change anything. Inevitably this limits both the artistic process and the insight it could bring.

In contrast, when the creative process is permitted to be a valuable discipline in its own right, space is made for exploration, inquiry, discovery and new insight. Some artists describe this as the space through which grace enters to make art greater than the sum of its parts. It is this process that makes the difference between a forgettable piece of art and a living, vibrant, multi-layered work of art that speaks with depth and subtlety to many different people. [See Case Study 9]▶

Another reason that the reputation of contemporary art in churches is less than it could be is the uncomfortable reality that the church can sometimes be an uncritical home for artists. As Steve Scott says:

> There are many examples in the Christian subculture of poorly executed art propped up with appeals to the spirituality of the artist's intentions or, worse still, the Bible itself. This practice is dishonest and sets a disastrous precedent… The art makers insulate themselves from any critical discussion of their work and from genuine growth in their skills.[25]

Churches can compound this problem by settling for 'second best' through an honourable desire not to hurt people or a reluctance to voice a truth that may be painful to an artist. But most good artists are open to honest criticism. Their reputations are all-important for getting future work and they need to ensure that their work doesn't suffer by association with an institution that is uncritical. Of course good art can and does explore Christian or biblical themes with integrity and insight but it shouldn't need to appeal to 'the spirituality of the artist's intentions' for justification.

Linked to all these points is the thorny issue of money. Over 50 per cent of professional UK artists earn less than £5,000 a year from their art.[26] This is scandalously below the national minimum wage, and many talented artists are forced to abandon their artistic careers in order to earn enough money to survive. There is a crisis of patronage in the arts in general, and yet many churches expect professional artists, musicians, actors and dancers to donate their services for little or even no financial reward. Many otherwise willing artists do not accept invitations to work with churches simply because they know they cannot afford to.

Yet there are also excellent artists in churches who feel called to offer their creativity as a gift for ministry but find that their gift is neither valued

---

25 Steve Scott, *Like A House on Fire* (Chicago: Cornerstone Press, 1997), 64.
26 Matthew Rooke, *Creativity in Business* (Glasgow: Scottish Cultural Enterprise Ltd., August 2000), 1.

nor accepted beyond the traditional musical demands of a typical church service. In more extreme cases, some Christian communities have even been known to suggest that people who work successfully in the secular creative industries should find a 'more worthwhile' career.

What ends up happening as a consequence of these dynamics is that Christian artists learn to avoid potential tensions by choosing to attend churches that already have a track record of welcoming creative talent; where their gifts are valued and they feel respected as whole people. Some churches become blessed with an abundance of creative people while others end up with none.[27]

It sometimes seems hard to get the balance right: to welcome and value artists while being discerning about their work; to accept the offer of their gifts for the service of God while not taking advantage of people who may be struggling financially; to give enough professional freedom to artists while ensuring that they have respect for wider sensitivities in the church. Yet these are already issues that churches deal with when employing Christians in the service industries (for example, architects or teachers). What is clear is that the potential benefits to both artist(s) and church are so great that it is worth putting in the time and energy and prayer to get it right.

3.2 Professional and amateur

It is important that a church can trust the skills and experience of any artist or artistic company it plans to work with. This doesn't mean that the artist(s) must be professional or that a church shouldn't use the artists in its midst. It does mean that the process of deciding to work with an artist needs to be transparent, professionally handled and supported by prayer. This ensures that even before it has begun a project is already in a good position to inspire collective optimism, confidence and support. [See Case Study 3]▶

In general, it is advisable for a church that has not had experience of running artistic projects to consider introducing professional artists – at least to get things started. This has a number of benefits. It ensures that the church's first experience of engaging with the arts is of good quality and standard. If your first project is a disaster, it is unlikely to become a springboard for a

---

27 The issue of spiritual gifting and discernment within Christian communities (arising from 1 Corinthians 12–14) is like a two-edged sword. On the one hand, churches need to ensure that they have a place for artistic gifts; on the other hand, churches need to be discerning as to who, in fact, has been artistically gifted (see below).

glorious new creative ministry. If you already have talented artists in your congregation, they should certainly be involved, but it may be a wiser long-term option to ensure that they don't have to bear the sole responsibility for the church's first major artistic venture. If some members of your congregation need persuading as to the value of the arts, they may be more receptive to an outsider with recognized credentials. You may find, too, that professional artists who are experienced at working with churches are already alert to potential opportunities and threats and are equipped to deal with them.

The issue of professional employment of artists can be a sensitive one if your church is not wealthy. The tempting solution might be to engage an artist who will work in your church for little or no money. While many successful artistic projects have been undertaken in this way, there are a number of practical and moral issues to bear in mind before doing this with a clear conscience:

> Christian artists often rely on the work they get from churches for part or all of their income. They are often poorly paid and motivated by faith and commitment rather than financial gain. It is unfair to prey on their willingness to perform their ministry for free if you can afford to pay them.

> The role of an artist may be valued less by your church if it costs nothing. Sacrificial giving of time or money in order to pay an artist might be a valuable part of the overall project. An informal, non-professional arrangement between church and artist leaves both vulnerable to lack of commitment and misunderstanding.

> Artists' fees do not have to be huge. In general, the arts offer excellent value for money and many artists will be flexible in their charges if they know your financial situation. It is often better to invest what you can in the spirit of the Parable of the Talents (*Matthew 25: 14–30*) than to skimp on fees and jeopardize the future of both your artist and your project.

Some of the practical considerations concerning employment of artists (planning, finding artists, issuing contracts, setting fees, etc.) are dealt with in the next section of this book. Whether you are looking to enrich the ministry of your church through artists in your midst, or to experiment with something completely new by engaging external artists, the process is bound to bring you joy, exhilaration and the reward of 'a music that you never knew to listen for'.[28]

---

28 Seamus Heaney, 'The Rainstick' from *Spirit Level* (London: Faber & Faber, 1996).

Section 2

Plans and Practical Advice

Section 2. Constructing set and staging needs hard work and patience (photo: Jeremy Begbie, TTA).

4

The Plan

Those who plan what is good find love and faithulfness
(Proverbs 14: 22)

As with most things, good planning is often the factor that makes the difference between a worthwhile artistic project and one that disappoints. Planning is not only an essential element in ensuring the success of a project; it can also be an exercise of disciplined thought and prayer that is valuable in its own right.

> It was the process of praying and planning together, learning new discipline and opening ourselves up to God's prompting which really released creative talents and changed lives.[29]

Planning need not be as daunting a process as it sometimes sounds. It is a means of thinking ahead to ensure that the best use is made of the available resources (time, money, people, buildings and equipment). These skills, of course, are no different to those involved in planning a normal service of worship. You may find, though, that planning an arts project demands a more formal approach, especially if you are to make funding applications, or satisfy the legal requirements for events which people pay to attend. If this is the case, you would be wise to think about the project so as to articulate the –

Aim(s): Why is this project worth doing? What do you hope to achieve?

Objectives: How do you plan to achieve the aim(s) over a set period of time?

Plan: How are your resources (time, money, people, buildings and equipment) to be gathered and co-ordinated to achieve the aims and objectives?

---

29 In conversation with Annette Aubrey, Babylon Bridge Dance Project.

This process will allow you to define and communicate the project. Potential weaknesses or problems can be dealt with before they become a threat. Potential supporters can gain a better understanding of the overall vision. Most importantly, at the end of the project you will be able to judge your achievements against the original plan and decide which elements are worth developing for the future. **[See Case Studies 2, 5 and 6]▶**

4.1 A basic plan

- Decide what you want to achieve and how you want to achieve it (aims and objectives).

- Bring together a planning group who share a commitment to realising the aims and objectives.

- Carry out a S.W.O.T. analysis (strengths, weaknesses, opportunities and threats) to determine what factors affect your church and your proposed project.

- Gather useful information that could support your planning and your projections (for example, publicity or planning documents from comparable projects).

- Determine a realistic time-frame for the project.

- Produce an itemized budget for projected income and expenditure (see Chapter 3).

- Produce a written plan (see below).

- Obtain the necessary permission and support to allow your plan to be put into action.

4.2 What to include

If you intend to use your plan to support funding applications, you may want to produce an (additional) full 'in house' version with the details and checklists for the entire project. Funding bodies are unlikely to wade through unnecessary detail, so a shorter version, with just the information relevant to them can be created from the key strategic elements.

Full Plan for Project Management	Condensed Plan for Funding Applications
Introduction (your church, its current situation)	Introduction (your church, its current situation)
S.W.O.T. analysis	Aims or goals (what you hope to achieve)
Aims or goals (what you hope to achieve)	Objectives (how you hope to get there)
Objectives (how you hope to get there)	Rationale (why the project is important and worth supporting)
Rationale (why the project is important and worth supporting)	Budget
Budget	Summary of key points
Checklist (individual tasks, who will do them and by when)	
Summary of key points	

4.3 Using your space

Churches are not always the easiest spaces for exhibitions or performances. Artistic additions to a church need to work in harmony with the architectural and other visual elements of the church building, as well as being consistent with the normal use of the building for worship.

You may need to think carefully about the practicalities of running your project in the space you have available. There are three options.

- You can tailor the project to the space and facilities you have.

- You can change your space (within reason) to accommodate the project.

- You can hire a different space.

The implications of each of these options will be unique to your church and project and will need to form part of your planning. Advice on the best use of your space can be sought from equipment hire companies, the Arts Council, the Council for the Care of Churches and from the artist(s) who will be involved in your project. [See Case Studies 2 and 5]▶

5

The Money

Money is like a sixth sense without which you cannot
make a complete use of the other five
(W. Somerset Maugham)

The more detailed you can make your projected budget, the more likely it is to give you a true picture of what your actual income and expenditure will be. Even if you have never run an arts event before, some basic research should give you a realistic impression of the income and expenditure you can expect. The best resource available is other people who have run similar projects.

Make sure that your budget includes any voluntary or donated contributions, including telephone calls, letter writing, free advice or services, costumes, props, decorations, food, equipment, etc. This will ensure that:

- people are properly acknowledged for their help,

- the true overall cost is recorded in case future projects or developments are undertaken, and

- the level of enthusiasm and sacrificial commitment for the project is indicated to potential funders.

5.1 Expenditure

A. *General principles*

Always plan pessimistically rather than optimistically. Underestimate income and overestimate expenditure. Allow a contingency sum for unforeseen expenses. This is usually 10 per cent of the total expenditure.

B. Artists' fees

Always make sure before you confirm a booking with an artist or an arts group that you know exactly how much you will be charged. This will include not only the artistic fee, but also the cost of any equipment, staging, lighting or display requirements. It is also wise to make sure that travel and accommodation expenses are agreed beforehand. If you have budgeted for basic 'bed and breakfast' accommodation and your artist charges you for accommodation in a luxury hotel, you could suddenly find yourself with a financial problem. Different artists will charge very different fees, depending on:

- the cost to them of your project (for example, a sculpture workshop will generally cost more than a poetry workshop because of the materials required);
- the amount of time the artist requires for preparation and participation;
- the popularity of the person or group you are booking;
- the number of artists taking part.

Most artists and groups will be able to give you an itemized quote for your proposed project. If you want advice on charges, you can contact the Arts Council for your region (addresses in the Resource Section at the end of this book).

C. Equipment hire

You can always get quotes from equipment hire companies. Some have special rates for charitable organizations or for educational projects. It is always worth asking about special deals. If your technical requirements are complex (for example, co-ordinated multi-media displays), you may need to hire the expertise of a professional to set up and /or operate the equipment. This sometimes reduces the cost of insurance but will increase the overall cost of hire.

You may also need to rehearse with equipment, which will increase the period of hire and may have implications for the normal use of the space involved. All this will need to be taken into consideration for your budget.

D. Publicity costs

If attracting an audience is an important element for your project, it would be wise to allocate at least 10 – 20 per cent of the overall budget for promotion and publicity. Publicity material, programmes and educational material can all be very expensive. Printing costs are dependent on:

- design time and complexity of machinery set-up for your print job;

- amount of paper being used;

- quality of paper;

- number of colours used.

For example, a full-colour leaflet cut to an unusual shape on heavy-weight paper will be very expensive to produce.

   You can save a lot of money by supplying pre-designed material on computer disk or as a camera-ready printout (check which format / computer programme your printing company uses) and by limiting the design to one or two colours. It is also worth remembering that leaflets and booklets, unlike posters and flyers (mini-posters), do not incur VAT.

   There are two ways of calculating the quantity of a minimum print run for leaflets promoting an event:

> For an event of limited capacity (for example, a performance), multiply by ten the total number of people you want to attend your event.

> For an event of unlimited capacity (for example an art exhibition), multiply by ten the number of people in your regular congregation. Add to this figure the number of leaflets you expect to distribute through other means (for example, libraries, schools, arts venues and other distribution facilities in your area).

It is always better to produce a little too much printed material than too little. Additional print runs cost more than printing an extra quantity first time around.

   Leaflets that can double-up as posters are sometimes a good idea. They will cost less to produce (as they can be included in a single print-job), they will not be subject to VAT and they will be more versatile if you are not sure about the proportion of posters to leaflets that you require.

   Make sure your print and design budget includes costs like advertising, display material, signage and distribution.

5.2 Income

There are various sources you can turn to for funding your venture. The first and most obvious is the income generating potential of the event itself. The second is the support base your project already has. The third is an external appeal for grants and sponsorship.

A. Income-generating

i) Ticket sales

Setting ticket prices can be difficult, especially when your arts project is intended to offer an accessible glimpse of Christian life to the unchurched. If your prices are too expensive, you will be excluding people who might benefit from the event. If your prices are too cheap, this will make your fund-raising task more difficult and possibly devalue the experience you offer. It is easy to do some basic research into ticket prices for comparable events. You could also conduct an informal opinion poll with your congregation. Describe the event and ask what people would consider a fair price.

One way to project ticket income for your budget is to multiply 60 per cent of the maximum audience capacity by the average price of tickets. This method assumes that you have an effective publicity strategy and that maximum audience figures and ticket pricing are realistic.

For example: you are planning a play with an audience capacity of 200 per night running for 2 nights at a cost of £5 for adults and £3 for children, students, pensioners and the unwaged. Maximum audience capacity would be 400; average ticket price would be £4. Sixty per cent of 400 is 240 and 240 × £4 is £960. Thus £960 would be the figure entered in the 'Income' section of the projected budget.

If you choose to sell tickets through a public box office (some theatres, cinemas and local authorities provide this service), make sure you deduct from your projected ticket income the appropriate percentage off ticket sales and any other commission or fees.

One approach adopted by a number of arts organizations is a 'free ticketing' system. It is designed to encourage people to try out something new without pre-paying for something they may dislike and without compromising on ticket price. Tickets are made available free of charge on the understanding that audience members will be expected to make a voluntary payment at the end of the event based on the value they place on the experience. Surprisingly, this method has been shown to work extremely well for experimental events, usually yielding more than would be anticipated by setting a low ticket price to encourage new attendance. It requires a high level of confidence that the event will live up to expectations and a flexible approach to projecting ticket income. [See Case Study 2]▶

ii) Programmes and advertising

Programme sales are less controversial than ticket sales and may be a way of guaranteeing an income from an event. If you can demonstrate that the programme will be seen by a significant number of potential customers, you may be able to cover some or all of your print costs by selling advertising space in the programme (remember that advertising space will increase the print costs). The more expensive you make your programmes, the more people will share them among themselves. You can project a programme income by multiplying 30 per cent of maximum audience capacity by the sales price of one programme.

iii) Food and Drink

Commercial cinemas make around 70 per cent of their total income through sales of popcorn, sweets, snacks and soft drinks. This is because:

- people are prepared to pay a premium for refreshments at an event;
- the cinemas make good use of the 'dead' time between the time when people buy a ticket and the time when the film actually begins.

Make sure that any food and drink sales comply with food hygiene regulations, licensing legislation and any restrictions operating in your church. Some churches, for example, forbid alcohol consumption on the premises. You will also need to ensure that you have plenty of people selling refreshments to cope with the inevitable rush if purchasing time is restricted.

iv) Other sales

It may be that works of art, postcards, books, cds, videos and other merchandise associated with your event can be sold. For pre-existing material, it is best to purchase on a 'sale or return' basis. You will need to budget for expenditure (wholesale unit costs, postage, cash boxes, etc.) as well as any income made through sales. Check the recommended retail price for each item and make sure that you are aware of any tax liabilities that may arise. Individual suppliers or your local tax office should be able to advise.

B. Internal funding sources

There are a wide variety of funding sources that may help finance your project. Any professional fund-raiser will tell you that fund raising through existing contacts is much more likely to be successful than an approach to someone who has no idea who you are. As a church activity, your project already has a significant potential resource in the form of your congregation. You may well have people in the congregation linked to trusts and foundations, wealthy individuals, arts funding bodies and local businesses. Your church may even have a budget for events and activities that enrich the life and faith of its congregation and wider community.

The most immediate sources of funding available to individual churches are:

	Advantages	Disadvantages
Church funds	– may be readily available	– may not be enough
	– will indicate the church's overall commitment to the project	– may decrease money available for other church projects
Members of the congregation	– will indicate high level of interest in and ownership of project	– may put unfair pressure on some members of congregation – may make it impossible to charge for the event
Fund-raising activities	– will generate money specifically earmarked for the project	– may exhaust time and energy before the project itself begins

C. External funding sources

Successful applications to external funding sources demand time spent in research and paperwork. Competition for grants is high, so applications need to be of a high standard, demonstrating the real and distinctive value of the proposed project.

The first step is to discover whether people in your congregation have contacts or expertise in fund raising. Sources include:

- Grants from public sources (Local government arts/culture/heritage funds, Arts Council or Regional Arts Board funds);

- Grants from trusts and foundations;

- Sponsorship from the corporate and business sector.

If you do find contacts in this way, you would be wise to involve them in any approach you decide to make to the organization(s) with which they have links.

The second step is to discover which sources your project is eligible for. There is little point applying to an organization whose primary interests lie outside the aims of your project. Basic research into this can be carried out in the following ways:

Source	Research
Public sources	A simple telephone call (see the Resource Section of this booklet for the main contacts) will usually determine your eligibility for public sources. The National Lottery, The Arts Councils (of England, Wales, Scotland and Northern Ireland), Regional Arts Boards and local authorities all publish free application guidelines for the funding schemes they operate. You may wish to consult these before speaking in detail to the organization concerned.
Trusts and foundations	Lists of eligibility criteria, grants and special funds are listed in a number of publications (details in the Resource Section). *The Directory of Grant Making Trusts* (Charities Aid Foundation, ISBN 0 904757 99 4) is an excellent starting point, listing more than 3,000 trusts and their primary areas of giving. It is updated annually and your library should be able to obtain a copy if it does not already have one.
Sponsorship	Knowledge of the interests of local companies can be obtained through employees and the local press. Successful sponsorship arrangements have obvious benefits for both parties, so you need to find companies who would benefit from being associated with your project, or who might want to make contact with your congregation or audience. You will also need to be careful about the image a sponsorship arrangement creates for your project. (A healthy-living project is unlikely to want sponsorship from a tobacco company.)

In general, projects whose primary aim is Christian evangelism are unlikely to be eligible for public money (from e.g. the National Lottery, local government, Arts Council or Regional Arts Boards). If, however, your primary aim is to explore a wider issue through the arts (for example, war, world debt, women in ministry) you may be eligible for these sources. If professional artists or groups with a good track record are involved, this will often increase your chances of obtaining public money.

D. *Making an application*

Once you have determined the sources for which you are eligible to apply, it is a good idea to concentrate your efforts on eight to ten 'best fits' – that is, the sources whose aims and objectives fit most comfortably with those of your project. You will then be better placed to do some further research into these sources. You can telephone public bodies, trusts and foundations to obtain application forms (where they are required) and detailed guidelines. You can again search out links your congregation might have with individual trustees or board members for the sources you are targeting. Any direct advice or support you can obtain will help in making your application successful.

Try to make applications as brief and informative as possible. The sooner you can get your point across, the more your application will stand out from the hundreds of applications that cross the desks of most funding bodies. If an application form is supplied, it should be clear what information is required. If you are asked to structure the application information yourself, a list of the key planning elements to be included is listed in Chapter 2 above. Whatever form your application takes, a potential funder will want to know:

What is this project?

Who is running it?

Why are they running it?

When will it happen?

How much would it cost?

Why should I/we support it?

When you have completed your application, it is a good idea to get at least two other people to read it for first impressions and clarity (as well as any obvious mistakes). Check how many copies the potential funder requires before sending it off.

You should receive notification whether your application is successful or not. It sometimes takes several months to get a reply from trusts and foundations. Most can tell you when a decision concerning your application will be made, although you may have to request this information.

If funding for the arts in churches is to increase in the long term, it is important that funders can trust churches to be wise stewards of their money. Many successful applications are followed by total silence from beneficiaries, even when basic reports and accounts are requested. If your funding application is successful, it is essential to nurture a good relationship with your supporters. Try to find out how they would like to be credited on your publicity and programmes. If you update them on your progress and invite them to see the fruits of their donation, you will be a good witness to the benefits of funding the arts in churches.

6

The Artist

6.1 Finding the right person

When looking at your project plan, is it obvious what kinds of qualities you are looking for in an artist? It is often a good idea to make some initial decisions about what sort of person or group would be most appropriate. These can be compiled into a 'wish list'. For example:

- Does it matter what art form the artist(s) practise(s)? Are you looking for a sculptor, a theatre group, a poet or are there several art forms you would consider?

- Does your artist need to be a good communicator? Do you want a simple performance/exhibit or are you going to ask them to speak about their work?

- Do you want your artist(s) to run workshops? If so, for which ages/interest groups in the church? Do you need to find an artist with experience as a teacher/facilitator?

- Do you have a particular theme in mind? If so, are you looking for an artist with a particular interest or expertise in this area?

- Does the faith or denomination of your artist(s) matter? Non-Christian artists may bring unexpected and fresh insights to a biblical text, for example, but you may want your project to start from an orthodox Christian perspective.

- Do you want to make a special effort to attract artists of diverse ethnic or social backgrounds?[30] The influence of different cultures may enrich your project.

---

30 Equal Opportunities legislation forbids discrimination on the grounds of racial or social background, colour, religion, disability or sex. Therefore, you can encourage application from social minority groups but you cannot make employment conditional on these criteria.

- How much time will you want your artist(s) to spend with your church? Does this put geographical limits on where your search should be based?

- How much money (lower and upper limits) are you prepared to pay your artist(s)?

When you have compiled your list, it can be combined with your aims and objectives to form a search document.

Search Document

[date]

[address]

[contact details]

St Andrew's Church is looking for a dancer, sculptor and poet to work together on a project designed to help people of all ages in our congregation to think more deeply about God as father, son and spirit.

We are a congregation of around 100 people of all ages and a variety of racial backgrounds. The church is situated in a busy high street and has a particularly active ministry among 14–25 year olds.

We would like to receive a curriculum vitae (with portfolio material where appropriate) and names of two referees from any dancer, sculptor or poet who:

is a good communicator;

has experience of running workshops;

has experience of working with other artists and enjoys working collaboratively;

has a sympathy with orthodox Christian faith;

has a personal interest in the theme of this project.

The project is intended to run over three consecutive weekends (August 12/13, 19/20 and 26/27) culminating in a public performance on the evening of August 28 resulting from the previous sessions.

A fee of £1,000 per artist plus travel and accommodation (B&B) expenses will be paid.

Deadline for information and applications is 20 February.

Applications are welcome from dancers, sculptors and poets of any ethnic background.

Once you have compiled your search document, it can be circulated to any source you think might be able to recommend suitable artists. Regional Arts Boards, the Arts Council, the Internet, newspapers, libraries, university art departments, colleges of art and local authorities are all good places to start. Some good sources for finding Christian artists are: the Arts Centre Group, Arts in Mission Resource Directory, churches that have run similar projects, and the Internet.

This process need not be complicated or time-consuming. A few well-placed phone-calls and some recommendations from friends could give you a list of artists to approach directly. Artists are used to being contacted in this way and will be happy to supply the information you want if they are interested in your project.

When you have chased up as much information as possible, you can shortlist the five or so artists or groups who seem most suitable. Basic information (excluding any confidential information) about these artists could then be presented at a church meeting and the shortlist pared down to a final two or three artists who can then be interviewed.

Be prepared to be surprised. Unexpected artists or groups may come to light and recommendations may come from unusual sources. [**See Case Study 6**]▶

6.2 Issuing a contract

Once you have selected your artist(s), it is wise to put your relationship on a professional footing. This is essential if any financial transaction is to take place. Some artists and groups will already have basic contracts for you to fill in with the details of your project. You may want to get this checked over by a solicitor before signing. If you are to draw up the contract yourself, make sure you include every aspect of the relationship that has been discussed. The Arts Council, your Regional Arts Board, and your library will have examples of contracts for you to see. They are usually very straightforward. Do consult a solicitor if you have any anxieties about issuing or signing a legally binding document.

7

The Audience

7.1 A secret weapon

If your project is to have a public dimension of any kind, you will need to spread the word about it as cheaply and effectively as possible. This will be particularly true if one of your aims is to bring new people into the church.

As a church, you already have access to the best promotional resource known to marketers, and it won't cost any money. People! Any advertiser will tell you that word of mouth promotion from enthusiastic individuals is easily the most effective method of promoting anything from art to artichokes, from dance to deodorant. [**See Case Study 2**]▶

If there is a good chance that your project will bring new or non-Christian visitors to your church, their experience of the church before, during and after the event is likely to have an influence on their opinion of your church, the wider church and even Christianity in general. There are some aspects of this process that you cannot influence, but your marketing and publicity strategy can be designed so that you make it as easy as possible for new visitors to feel comfortable about coming to your church. This is an opportunity to enhance the impact of your project by making the whole experience a good one.

7.2 Marketing strategy

Say 'publicity' to most people and they think of leaflets, posters and newspaper articles. These are certainly good publicity tools but they may or may not be appropriate for your event. Spending money on these is worth while only if you are sure they will work.

Before you think about any printed material, you need to be clear about what you are communicating, who you are communicating it to and why.

Your decisions about how you do this will be more effective if you have answered these three important questions.

- What are you 'selling'? What parts of the project do you need to communicate? What will people need to know?

- Who are you aiming at? Are they Christian or not, how old are they, what sorts of things do they enjoy doing, what are their interests, what would encourage or hinder their participation?

- Why are you promoting the project? What do you hope to achieve? If you hope to attract an audience, how many people do you want? If you want to raise awareness about your church or its activities, how do you want people to act on this information?

When you have answered these questions, you can begin to imagine your event from the perspective of the people you hope to attract. If you were one of them, how would you find information about events? What would make you want to attend something? What would make you actually attend something? What practical factors might make attendance easier or more difficult?

Based on this approach, you can begin to set the flavour of your publicity campaign. For example, the overall image could be fun, thought provoking, funky, witty, challenging, sophisticated, bold, energetic, tranquil, contemplative, new, familiar or a combination of these and other qualities.

You could also sum up your project with a title or slogan reflecting the kind of event, such as:

> *Art in the Park – a family fun day with workshops for all ages*
>
> *Who is God? – a Christian meditation in words, movement and sculpture*
>
> *War and Pieces – a video and photography exhibition by young artists from Bosnia*
>
> *Noise – a new musical about life, death, sex … and church?*
>
> *Wild Child – no one listened to Jess until the day she learnt to dance*

7.3 Motivating the congregation

If your congregation has been involved in the planning process for an arts project and if the project itself is seen as part of the life and ministry of the church, you should already have a congregation that is at least sympathetic to its aims and objectives. In order to turn general goodwill into effective promotion, the following may help:

- Make sure the church leaders support the project. If they give public endorsement to the project, this will establish it as a valued church activity.

- Make sure that members of the congregation know how to describe the project to other people. Printed material and regular announcements in services can help. Announcements could be presented in the style of the project itself, with props, costumes, music or educational elements.

- If there are regular aspects to a project (for example, a series of workshops), perhaps a teaching slot in the service or in the Sunday School could be set aside to include the congregation in the project's progress.

- Setting targets can clarify what you hope members of the congregation will do. For example, every member of the congregation could be encouraged to tell at least five other families about an event.

- Distribution of information will be easy if tasks are allocated according to people's usual routine. For example, teachers and parents can distribute information in schools, and members of sports teams or gyms can put posters up in sports centres.

- You could operate reward systems for good promoters – e.g. buy four tickets, get one free. [See Case Study 5]▶

7.4 Young people

If one of the aims of your project is to reach young people, it might be worth making a special effort to ensure that the method and style of your publicity campaign is likely to be effective. Generally speaking, young people tend to be amazingly discerning about what they will or won't respond to. They are so used to receiving information in visual forms that they will soon spot inconsistencies of image and text.

You may find that by being involved, young people will happily spread the word among their peers. On the other hand, if they are at all embarrassed by what's on offer, they won't want anyone to know about it, least of all their peers.

Methods of reaching young people vary from area to area. You may find that the local radio has more credibility but less catchment than information circulated via schools. 'What's On' listings in leaflets or on the web may or may not have a youth readership.

As with all publicity, if you can inspire enthusiasm among a few key individuals, word of mouth promotion is the most effective way of spreading the news. If you can inspire a few people whose opinion is trusted (other young people, youth leaders, radio DJs, celebrities, teachers, etc.), this may be your best strategy. [**See Case Study 7**]▶

7.5 Publicity tools

A. *Text*

Text-based material can take many forms. Leaflets and posters are the most common, but sometimes more quirky methods can get the point across just as cheaply and are less likely to end up in the dustbin. For example, pencils, mug mats, postcards, bookmarks, paper aeroplanes, the Internet and even fabric can all be vehicles for your information. Your local 'yellow pages' should have details of companies who produce 'promotional gifts'. If the method you use reflects the style and nature of your project, it can say more than paragraphs of text. For example, black and silver pencils printed with the event and ticket details recently helped generate a sell-out audience for a Christian poetry and dance event entitled 'Getting the Point Across'.

Whatever format you adopt, your text-based information should always include title, place, date, time and contact details. It also needs to be:

- accurate – in terms of spelling, grammar and information;
- consistent – with an agreed format for dates, times, fonts and key phrases;
- simple – free of jargon and long sentences;
- interesting – with fresh ideas and images rather than clichés;
- clear – with font sizes and colours clear enough for older eyes;
- easy to follow – clearly stating what those wanting to attend need to do.

In order to assess your writing style, try reading your text aloud. If you have to pause for breath mid-sentence, your sentences may be too long. If you have to re-read something, it may be unclear. Ask someone who has not been involved in planning the event to read it through for accuracy and clarity.

B. The Internet

The Internet has become an important source of events information. If your church already has a web site, it should be easy to add an event or exhibition to the site. This will not be an effective promotional tool, however, unless people who might be interested in attending can access the information. An hour or so surfing the web for 'what's on' sites for your area and for church-based activities should give you an idea of the sites from which your information needs to be accessible. Most sites of this kind will provide you with the instructions you need to ensure that your information can be reached through them.

C. The press

The local, regional or national press may be interested in your project and you may feel that press coverage could benefit your church and your project.

i) Advertising

Press advertising can be expensive but it is a good way to ensure that an event or exhibition is listed in the usual 'events' section of your local paper and/or your local 'what's on' magazine. Many paid press adverts will include your event on Internet listings for your area. Some local papers provide all their listing services for free.

ii) Media releases

If you think your project would be of interest to your local paper, regional television and radio, the church press or the national press, you could produce a media release. Most editors are inundated with information, so your media release will be most effective if it is eye-catching, brief, informative and has a good 'story' which will be of interest to readers, listeners or viewers. The mere existence of your project is unlikely to make a good story by itself. You need to look for something interesting, famous or quirky that might capture an editor's imagination. 'Rainforest band drum up support at St Martin's', 'Poet Laureate joins Sunday school', or 'Vicar learns to dance' might work.

Media releases normally comprise a single, one-sided sheet of A4 paper. Use the church's headed notepaper if you can. Otherwise, add the church's details to the page yourself including the date and 'Media Release' or 'Press Release' at the top of the page.

Give the story a simple, eye-catching title and add 'with picture' if you are sending a photograph.

The body text should be well spaced with wide margins and should describe the who, where, what, why and when of your project in as interesting a way as possible.

At the end of the main text, write 'ends' and then include your contact information (including telephone number, fax and e-mail) and a caption and names for any photograph.

Make sure that you send your media release in good time for the relevant editorial deadlines.

7.6 Making it easy

If you have been successful in attracting general interest in your project, you then need to make sure that it is easy for people to attend and that their experience in coming to your church will be a good one.

> Is it straightforward to buy tickets?

> Are there practical details that wheelchair users, the hard of hearing, the partially sighted or families with young children will need to know about?

> Do you have good signage to direct people who have not visited your church before?

> Do you have enough helpers to make sure that things will run as smoothly as possible and everyone will feel welcomed?

8

The Law

If there were no bad people
there would be no good lawyers
(Charles Dickens)

Even Jesus might have fallen foul of current UK public events legislation. UK law prohibits any event which is 'obscene, incites racial hatred or provokes a breach of the peace'. (Table turning in the temple would certainly have transgressed the third category.) Even the Church of England canon demands that any event occurring in a church should be 'suitable' for its ecclesiastical environment.[31]

Although you may not be planning to breach either the peace or the codes of suitable conduct relating to your church or denomination, the legal side of running events can still be a minefield. As with all issues concerning event co-ordination, planning is the key. The legal principles make good sense and are designed to protect artists, promoters and the general public.

Churches are already well placed to meet many of the legal requirements for running an event. Most churches already have charitable status, which solves many of the issues concerning non-profitmaking events. Any building used for public worship should already have most of the necessary insurance cover. All groups using music regularly in worship should be registered with Christian Copyright Licensing, and many churches are already registered with the Performing Rights Society. If you are in doubt about the status of your church with regard to any of these issues, you should be able to check with the person responsible for legal and financial issues in your church. If you are still in doubt, you can contact the individual bodies as listed in the Resource Section of this book below. They are all very approachable and are used to dealing with questions from first-time event organizers.

---

31 Canon F16 of *Church of England Canon Law*.

8.1 Insurance

Any building used for public worship should already have the following insurance:

- public liability – for people coming into the building or participating in events;

- building contents;

- equipment;

- personal accident cover.

If you are bringing new equipment into the building either temporarily or permanently, you will need to check that this is covered by either its owner(s), or by the church's existing insurance company. An extension of cover may well be required for visual art exhibits, technical equipment or large props. Of course, any extra insurance cover required will need to be added onto the project budget.

8.2 Safety

Event promoters (including churches) have a legal and moral responsibility for the safety of the public while on their premises. Churches are not usually considered high-risk places, but if you are running an event which will change the usual access or fire escape routes, or which might have safety implications (for example, flammable materials, heavy objects, etc.) it may be worth consulting a health and safety officer from your local council. Safety issues in your church may also be specific to your audience group. For example, there will be specific safety issues for an event involving small children as either participants or audience. If you can demonstrate that you have taken proper account of safety in your planning process, this should prevent accidents and provide a safeguard against being held responsible if something does go wrong.

Most churches that run children's education programmes will already be familiar with legislation relating to the supervision of children. Rules and guidelines are under constant revision to ensure that vulnerable children are protected whenever they are being supervised by people other than their parents or legal guardians. If you plan to run activities for children, it is essential that you comply with the appropriate legislation. To secure the most up-to-date information, guidelines, and interpretation you are advised to contact your church organization's head office (or equivalent), your local authority, or government education department. Each should be able to advise you on law and regulation relating to children and those who work with them in a voluntary or paid capacity.

8.3 Value Added Tax

Churches have no special status under law regarding VAT. They are treated for tax purposes like any other charitable organization. Assuming that your church is not VAT registered (most are not), you will not have to charge VAT on any ticket prices for events you run. If your church is VAT registered, you will need to charge VAT on tickets, and perhaps on some other sources of income, but you may be able to claim VAT back on expenditure. For example, VAT should be levied on sponsorship in which the sponsor benefits from the relationship (including sponsorship in kind). A grant or donation, however, is exempt from VAT. If you are in doubt about your VAT registration status, or about specific transactions, you should contact your local HM Customs and Excise office.

8.4 Licences

One or more licences may be required for your church or church hall if you plan to run an event that could be classed as a 'public performance'. Licences exist to ensure the safety of the general public in specific buildings. Different councils vary on their interpretation of licensing laws. An act of worship will not usually require a licence (but will require copyright legislation to be met; see below). A ticketed event that is open to the general public, however, is likely to require a licence. The good news is that licences are generally free of charge for performances of an educational or religious nature and those performed for a charitable purpose (which usually includes events where any profit goes to charity).

A. Public Entertainment Licence

A P.E.L. can be granted on an annual or an occasional basis.

> *Required for:* places used for public dancing, music and public displays; (music played in churches does not require a Public Entertainment Licence).

Covers: fire and safety, hygiene, hours of use for public enter-tainment, numbers of people allowed on premises, provision of super-vision.

Contact: Local Authority.

Notice needed: 28 days.

B. *Theatre licence*

A theatre licence can be granted on an annual or an occasional basis.

Required for: stage performances (play, ballet, opera or similar).

Covers: similar to P.E.L., plus seating arrangements and other issues specific to stage performances.

Contact: Local Authority.

Notice needed: 14 days.

C. *Film and video licences*

It is unlikely that a film or video licence will be needed for most church activities or events, but you may need to notify your council or gain an exemption. In general:

No licence is required for a public showing if no admission charge is made.

No licence is required when an admission charge is made but the premises are not used for public film showing on more than six days in a year. (Although in this case, written notification of the showing needs to be made at least seven days beforehand to the local authority, fire and police services.)

No licence is required if the organization concerned has a Certificate of Exemption. These are available to non profit-making organizations from the Home Office. They are valid for 5 years. A small fee is payable and showings must not take place on more than 3 days in any 7-day period.

A licence is required for children's 'film clubs' unless the showings are part of the activities of an educational or religious institution.

8.5 Copyright

Copyright is one of the few channels through which musicians, authors and the organizations that represent them can be rewarded financially for their work. Considering the difficulty many professional Christian artists, musicians and authors have in raising a living income, it is short sighted and immoral (as well as illegal) that many churches breach copyright with an apparent lack of concern. If churches are to benefit from good quality new music, writing and art, they need to be committed to supporting this process and protecting artists by respecting copyright. Copyright currently operates during the life of a composer, artist or author and for 70 years from the end of the year of his or her death. It also operates for 50 years after the first issue of a recording.

A. *Christian Copyright Licensing*

Any organization that meets regularly for Christian worship (for example churches, schools, universities, and prisons) is already likely to posses a Christian Copyright licence. This covers the reproduction of words of songs of worship through overhead projection, printed material and recording.

The body which issues Christian Copyright licences also deals with granting special licenses for the video recording of worship material (for example, at weddings and baptisms).

Christian Copyright (Europe Ltd) can grant an occasional or an annual licence (address and telephone details are in the concluding Resource Section). Annual licences cost between £30 and £380 per year. The cost is dependent on the average weekly attendance at the place of worship. Each participating organization is asked to complete an annual return indicating the hymns and songs sung and their frequency. Song and hymn writers are then paid according to the overall use of their material.

B. *Performing Rights*

A Performing Rights licence is generally required for the live or recorded performance of any copyrighted music that is not covered by Christian Copyright. As with Christian Copyright, this can be as relevant to a service of worship as to an event.

The only exception to this would be the performance by a live group of their own material where they are not members of the Performing Rights Society.

Many churches already have a Performing Rights licence. In this case, the performance of music as part of an event can be added to the usual Performing Rights return. A programme and note of the net box office income will need to be included.

If you plan to have a musical performance and your church does not already have a Performing Rights licence, you will need to contact the Performing Rights Society (address in Resource Section). You may obtain either an annual licence for general use or a special permit for a one-off event.

Churches are normally invoiced for such performances (even if the event is for charitable purposes) on a quarterly basis. The amount charged is calculated on the basis of:

- 3.3 per cent of net box office income for classical music;

- the capacity of the church (where there is no box office income);

- 3 per cent of net box office income for pop, jazz and carols;

- 2 per cent of net box office income for events with dialogue and music.

C. Dramatic musical performances

Permission for the performance of operas, ballets, musicals, etc. should be sought from the composer, publisher or agent concerned. Scores usually give the name and address to which requests should be made.

D. Use of sound recordings

In addition to the right to perform music on a recording (covered by the Performing Rights Society), the recording itself is also covered by copyright. For church purposes, though, you may be relieved to know that a Phonographic Performance Licence is not required as long as the performance is part of the activities, or for the benefit of an organization whose main objects are charitable.

9 Building on Success

Let another praise you and not your own mouth
(Proverbs 27: 2)

9.1 The aftermath

The completion of an arts project is usually greeted with a sigh of relief! No matter how fantastic the outcome, it will have been demanding and sometimes stressful. Even if the project has not happened exactly as you envisaged, your foundation of prayer and good planning will have yielded benefits that may or may not be immediately apparent. [**See Case Studies 2 and 6]▶**

The discipline of winding up a project and deciding whether or how to build on areas of success is sometimes the last thing you want to be faced with in the immediate aftermath. Some tasks will definitely need to be carried out as soon after the project's end as possible, such as:

- paying artists, hire companies and any other invoices which are due;
- thanking helpers, organizers and funders;
- producing the final accounts;
- sending a report to funders and any other interested parties.

While you are carrying out these tasks, it would be a good time to take stock of what has happened and to document this in some form. The collective memory of a church can be limited and some tangible evidence of the project's life could be a valuable resource for future planning.

It is always good practice to debrief the people most heavily involved with running the event. A short, informal meeting (perhaps over a meal) is all that is needed. This is a good way of saying thank you while recording people's individual reactions concerning the project and praying for its ongoing legacy. A simple debriefing would try to determine the following points from each person's perspective:

What worked particularly well?

What was less successful?

What would you do again?

What would you do differently

Is follow-up work needed?

Is there an obvious way to build on the successes of the project?

This information can be used for the final report, as well as for future planning. It could be written up in simple point form for future reference.

9.2 Feedback

Another valuable tool for future planning is to seek feedback from those who took part and those who attended. Again, this need not be complicated or time consuming. There are various methods of getting feedback.

A. Questionnaires

These have the advantage of being very specific. You can ask exactly what you want to know about a person's reaction to the project. This information is then easy to quantify and collate for future reference. The potential disadvantages of this method are that it is sometimes difficult to get an overall impression and you may miss out on learning information not covered by the questionnaire. Unless you offer an incentive for returning the forms, you may find that not many people return them, or that those who take the trouble to fill them in have particularly strong opinions, distorting an accurate impression of what the 'silent majority' actually thought.

B. Opinion box

This is an unobtrusive way of collecting people's reactions over an extended period of time. It is anonymous and instant and gives people a chance to decide what they want to tell you. Like questionnaires, this method is self-selecting, so you may not get an accurate sense of majority opinions.

C. Visitor book

This is a traditional feature of exhibitions and reading other people's comments is part of the fun. Comments tend to be written with a wider audience in mind, so they are not ideal feedback tools but can provide a lively sense of the kinds of issues raised by an exhibition.

D. Verbal feedback

Verbal feedback can take many forms. Some organizations formalize the process by pre-selecting 'representatives' (people who represent different groups whose opinion is sought) to attend and then comment on an event or exhibition. These people are asked to take part with the knowledge that their detailed observations and opinions will be presented at a feedback meeting. Another approach is to ask someone to act as an informal interviewer, seeking opinions and comments from people during or after the project. If people are to be honest about their impressions it is important that the interviewer be perceived as independent from the organizational team.

9.3 The shape of things to come

Once you have determined which parts of your project were most valuable, and which were least successful, you will be in a good position to begin to think about where the next steps might lead. Your initial project could be the beginning of an ongoing artistic ministry in your church. It could catalyse a series of public events or it could encourage the congregation to use their talents more creatively in the general life of your church.

Whatever happens as a result of a prayerful, well-planned and well-integrated artistic venture in your church, you can be sure that by the grace of God new insights, new inspirations and new challenges will have changed lives.

phoenix

and yes
the greyest
ashes do
blaze again

given this
fresh fuel
this fusing
contact made

this match from
the kindling cross
phosphorously
lamping you

with impossible
new colour[32]

---

32 'phoenix' by Andrew Rumsey, *Homing In* (Carlisle: Paternoster, 1998), 43.

Section 3

Case Studies

Section 3. A 'hands-on' exploration of sculpture with work by Ernesto Neto, 2000. (copyright DCA, photo: Sarah Derrick).

1. Sounds of Scripture

Jeremy Begbie

Jeremy Begbie is Director of 'Theology Through the Arts' (Cambridge and St Andrews), Associate Principal of Ridley Hall (Cambridge), Affiliated Lecturer in the Faculty of Divinity, University of Cambridge and Reader at the University of St Andrews, in the newly-established Institute of Theology, Imagination and the Arts. A professionally trained musician, he has lectured extensively in 'theology through the arts' in the UK, North America and South Africa, through multi-media presentations. He is author of Music in God's Purposes *and* Voicing Creation's Praise: Towards a Theology of the Arts. *His most recent book,* Theology, Music and Time, *was published in 2000 by Cambridge University Press.*

A few years ago, I was asked to take a group of students from Ridley Hall to lead a weekend on music in worship. It was at a church situated deep in one of the leafier parts of south-east England. We were asked to rehearse singers and instrumentalists on the Saturday in preparation for a Sunday morning service. Always nervous of choirs and singers, I designed things so that I would spend most of it with the instrumentalists.

The church was large and well endowed, so I expected a fair number of players to turn up. But I never expected the variety which greeted me – two flutes, a harp, a bassoon, a euphonium, a cello, two electric guitars, two synthesizers and a trumpet. Nor did I expect the age range which faced me – from a twelve-year old flautist to a 60-year old synthesizer player.

We spent the first part of Saturday morning rehearsing written arrangements. They were good players, but they obviously hadn't played together before and were hesitant and nervous. We got through the set pieces and then found we had an hour or so to spare.

I decided to risk an experiment. We would improvise on a biblical text. I chose Matthew 3 – the baptism of Jesus by John the Baptist. It is not especially well known but full of drama, and full of sounds.

I put copies of the text on their music stands. They looked dumbstruck. 'Where's the music?' they asked. 'In front of you,' I told them. I assured them I had not done this before, so I (as the pianist) was joining them in the same boat. All I would do is read the text aloud and ask questions about it as we improvised. I urged them to speak only when absolutely necessary.

As we started, I tried to avoid saying, 'Picture the scene.' I asked them instead to hear it. They were, after all, musicians. 'What does the wilderness sound like?' One of the keyboard players played a very low bottom C, with a huge, cavernous reverberation. The guitarists whined on their upper strings. And John the Baptist; what does he sound like?' The trumpeter – every inch the extrovert – walked to the other aide of the large church and let out a repeated fortissimo four-note motif which echoed around the building. 'What's the response?' 'Crowds flocked to hear him and were baptized.' One of the flautists asked what note the trumpet was playing. I asked her to listen and find out for herself, which she did. She began to improvise on the four-note motif. Soon other players joined her – like the crowds in the wilderness. We worked right through the passage. When we reached the point where Jesus comes on the scene, one of the synthesizers 'pulled up' the bottom C to an E flat, and spread out a chord on top of the E flat – the new age of Jesus was arriving. 'And what theme are we going to give Jesus?' The twelve-year old flautist responded: 'Why not turn the John Baptist theme upside down?' So she took the four-note motif and did just that. She had only been learning the flute for a few weeks. She had just learned a technique called 'inversion' and through it, helped us discover one of the main points of the passage. The coming of the Spirit upon Jesus was then improvised by all the players in the form of a remarkable 12-note chord, gradually swelling into a deafening climax, capturing perfectly the sense of fulfilment in the story.

When we had finished, the players were so elated they wanted to play their piece at the following morning's service. Sadly it was rejected because we couldn't give a guarantee of how long it would last.

What was going on that morning?

First, this was Bible study, through and through. It was not about getting away from Scripture into the world of music; just the opposite, it was about entering the world of the Bible through music. The players were glued to the text with the intensity of a biblical scholar.

Case study 1. Jeremy Begbie leads a workshop at St Edmundsbury Cathedral, Suffolk. 'Hearing is Believing', 14 November 1998 (photo: Pam Pitts).

Second, music was doing its own work in its own way – music has its own special powers to help us unlock and experience texts like this afresh.

Third, all the players could quickly take part because they were allowed to use a language that was natural to them – music. I doubt if that twelve-year old flautist would have said a word in a traditional Bible study. But with a flute in her hands she had music, and with music she had a language she knew. I am not recommending we reject more well-tried forms of Bible

study, only that we are sensitive to the different ways in which people naturally think, express themselves and communicate.

I have repeated this experiment in many contexts with many different
types of players. It can be done with singers, and in almost any art form.
But, presuming for the moment that it is done with instrumentalists, it
might be helpful to point out some practical matters which need to be
borne in mind.

- Allow plenty of time. Improvising will feel very strange to players (or
  singers) who normally play only with written music – and that is how
  most people are taught. Give them room to get used to it.

- If you are the leader, make sure you join in. Assure them you are taking
  the risk as well. This helps free everyone up to play an active role.

- Try to avoid telling them what to play. Let them interact with the text so
  the text can come alive through music in a way that is true to them. At
  times you may want to suggest things, but try to give them space.

- On the other hand, encourage them to think hard about when not to play.
  The secret of successful improvisation is learning when to stop and listen.

- Do not give them a commentary on the text – unless something is radically unclear. You will certainly need to read the text first, and you may
  want to talk about it together, but my preference has been to keep talk to
  a minimum in order to let music do its own work.

- Assure them it is perfectly acceptable to make mistakes, try things out and
  drop them if need be. This is improvisation, not a perfect performance.

If you can, persuade a church to let you contribute it to a service, with an
introduction explaining the underlying thoughts and process.

2. Cornerstone Arts Festival

Andrew Bonner

Andrew Bonner is an active member of St Silas' Church in Glasgow. In 1999, he and fellow-members of the church drama group had an idea for an event to mark the completion of some architectural work. It quickly developed a life of its own. Here is his account of what happened:

St. Silas is an evangelical Episcopal church in the West End of Glasgow; an area close to the city centre. It has a diverse congregation originating from all over the world and including university students, young graduates in temporary jobs, the elderly, arts and media professionals, homeless families living in temporary accommodation, people in the traditional professions and even a number of politicians and celebrities. There is a staff of four: one ordained minister, a pastoral assistant, an administrator, and a music co-ordinator. Around 150–200 people attend the two regular services: families and older people in the mornings, students and twenty-somethings in the evenings. Twelve house-groups meet mid-week.

The idea

Inspired by the success of all-age services at St. Silas, where sketches had been used extensively to illustrate Bible stories and ideas, the drama group volunteered to present a revue that would take an entertaining look at life in the church.

However, as soon as the idea took shape, it got bigger. Because Glasgow was UK Capital of Architecture and Design in 1999, and as the church was in the process of alterations, it was decided that the event could become our contribution to the city's special year. Why not involve lots of artists, working on different projects in the church? By timing everything to coincide with the completion of the alterations, this could be an event celebrating the church, its architecture and space, its love of the arts, the city in which we lived, and most importantly, Christ, the church's Cornerstone.

So the one-off revue quickly turned into a three-day festival. It would include a comedy-revue plus a new play, a dance drama, a children's musical event, a visual art installation along with an art exhibition, bands and musicians, percussion workshops, poetry-recitals, story-telling, and a special Sunday night service in which five members of the congregation would share the stories of how one significant work of art had shaped their personal growth in faith. Thus was the Cornerstone Festival born.

Planning and preparation

A steering group was formed some eight months before the event was due to take place. Each member of the group took responsibility for tasks such as financial planning, publicity and marketing, drama, dance, music, visual arts, church liaison, technical requirements and event safety/security. Initial meetings focused on festival content and explored what it was possible for a group of committed volunteers to achieve.

The steering group quickly realized that their planning would remain little more than a wish-list until funding could be secured. A budget was drawn up (based on a 50–60 per cent capacity audience for each event) and potential benefactors from within the church were approached. They agreed to underwrite the total cost of the festival.

To spread the cash burden, the steering group introduced an 'angels' / investors scheme in which members of the congregation bought £25 'shares' in the festival. They would receive a return on revenues raised, but were also warned that the festival involved some financial risk and that ultimately no money at all might be returned. In the event, they received most of their money back, but sadly, no profits.

Another key issue for the steering group was the controversial matter of entry fees. Charging for tickets would have turned the festival into a 'commercial operation', requiring prohibitively expensive licences from the local authority. Consequently, the group decided to ask for minimum dona-tions instead. Once the level of the donations had been set, and with the generous backing of benefactors and 'angels', the festival was finally secure and the preparations could begin in earnest.

The big event

As Cornerstone drew closer, the length and frequency of the meetings increased. Responsibilities grew and so did time commitments. This was easier for some of the steering group members than for others and, perhaps inevitably, some people ended up doing multiple tasks.

In the thirty-six hours before the festival, the church was filled with people bringing lighting and sound systems, chairs, tables, food, musical instruments, costumes, paintings and equipment borrowed from the city. Meanwhile, builders were finishing their alterations to the church while stage-designers built the set for the first production and performers sought somewhere quiet and uncluttered to nip and tuck performances.

It was a logistical mountain but somehow it was conquered with amazing efficiency and calm. All that planning came to life. Schedules swung into action. Everything managed to find a place and was on show at the times stated in our brochures.

Case study 2. A festival offers opportunities for everyone to get involved: Tent Event, Exeter, 1987 (photo: Sarah Derrick).

A huge number of people came through the church during the festival: it was in constant use, with arts events bulging from every corner. The highlight of the weekend came on Sunday evening, with the service, 'Celebrating the Cornerstone'. It was the key event of the festival, drawing together all that had taken place over the weekend: an opportunity to celebrate Christ through the arts, and a chance to explore what might be gained by allowing our imaginations to soar.

Lessons learned

The events were well attended (all were at least two-thirds full) but the festival would have made more overall sense if fewer events had been attempted over the three-day period. This would have spread organizers, performers and audiences less thinly and the 'angels' might even have made money.

Asking for donations instead of admission charges worked well. It was an accessible model that encouraged people to attend events that were new to them. People were happy to hand over their money, and we had no difficulty in justifying the levels set.

With so much to organize, the marketing suffered and we didn't capitalize fully on the project's ability to reach beyond the congregation. New people did come into the church, but more could have been reached. Next time we would spend more time and money on promotion.

Many were surprised at the high quality of the productions on offer. With hindsight, this reflects a lack of communication with the wider congregation. If they had realized the scale and quality of events, they might have been more engaged in the activities and more active in promoting them.

Lives changed

While there are things we would do differently next time, the overall operation was enriching, exciting and even life-changing for those involved.

The Saturday play, *Nobilissima Femina*, had a particular poignancy for those involved in its production. The play deals with the death of the main character's mother. By an extraordinary turn of events, the play was staged one week after the writer/director's mother died. He told how writing the play had prepared him to face some of the grief and the spiritual questions that were then raised by his mother's death. Joining him at the show was his father. The play became a God-given way for the writer to share both grief and hope with his father.

A year on, people are still talking about the events of the festival. For some, it was an opportunity to enjoy their faith in refreshing ways, for others it brought new and stimulating insight. For a few, it became the cornerstone for a new commitment to Christ.

3. In the Path of Bach:
the church as a patron of the arts

Katherine Freeze

University Presbyterian Church (UPC) in Seattle, USA has breathed new life into an artistic ministry that has a weighty historical track record. Some of the Western world's finest composers, including Bach and Mozart, were employed to compose music for churches that believed music to be an integral part of the worship life of the church community Katherine Freeze is the current Composer in Residence at UPC. She is a recent graduate in Music History and Theory from the University of Washington. UPC recognizes her role as being a valuable part of its overall ministry and welcomes the opportunity to support the development of a promising young composer.

The position that I currently hold at UPC (Composer in Residence and Associate Director of Sunday evening services) has its roots in a ministry begun in 1992 by a woman named Kari Medina. A classically trained pianist and composer, Kari, as a volunteer, took over the directorship of a fledgling Sunday Night 'contemporary' service. She assembled a team of singers, percussion players (bass, drums, guitars) and orchestral players (clarinet, flute, oboe, horn, cello, violin and viola). As she began to design worship services that integrated old and new worship and offertory material, she saw a need for music that was tailored to the specific players in her ensemble. She realized that music can be ineffective and irrelevant if it is poorly written or not authentic to the ensemble presenting it. As she searched for sacred music that would fit the needs of the music team, she saw that there was a scarcity of good, new, appropriate sacred music. Most was written for traditional ensembles (i.e. choir, orchestra, organ and soloists, etc.) and most was at best mediocre.

Kari identified the talents and the particular 'voice' of the eclectic ensemble at UPC and began writing music for it. She wrote some worship tunes, but mainly she wrote 'offertories'. She worked closely with the Senior Pastor, attempting to write music that complemented sermons. Kari's vision for a fully integrated service set a valuable new standard for the church, leading people to worship and ministering to them through word, teaching, music, and the presentation of a specially composed 'offertory' that reflects the overall design of each service.

I came to UPC first as a member of the student ministry called *The Inn*, playing piano and writing original songs for the worship team. When I graduated from the University of Washington in 1999, I started a year-long full-time internship in the worship department, working directly under Kari. She delegated writing projects to me, and I was also given the project of creating a new Christmas Eve service: a through-composed narration of the Christmas story with congregational carol singing and original pieces performed by our 18-piece ensemble. Other projects over the course of the year included composing, rehearsing and conducting a piece for choir and orchestra performed at the Lenten Concert, assisting with regular orchestra rehearsals, writing for an in-house concert and a variety of other tasks.

When Kari retired in May of 2000, the church decided to hire me to continue her composing and piano-accompanying duties (25 hrs/week). The directorship of what had become two Sunday Night services was entrusted to Catherine Hedberg, with whom I work closely.

As UPC began to realize the value and extent of Kari's work, they decided to make money available to pay her a salary. Congregational numbers were growing fast (we now have anywhere from 1200–1600 people on any given Sunday night), and the church decided that the ministry of music was a priority. My internship was funded by private donors and my present position is funded directly from the church, as Kari's was.

My duties within the church are as follows:

- Play the piano for two Sunday services (with appropriate rehearsals).

- Write orchestral parts for worship tunes (flute, clarinet, violin, cello, sometimes horn).

- Provide 'offertory' music (new compositions, new arrangements or music by special guests). This means meeting with pastoral staff, reading texts and other supplementary material, and then reflecting on it all in order to produce something interesting with musical integrity.

- Help with the cultivation of the music team (e-mailing, calling, meeting with them, writing for them, etc.).

- Lead rehearsals as necessary.

- Deputize for the Music Director as necessary.

In order to achieve all this, I try to stay connected and learn about our congregation so that I can write music that challenges and nourishes them. This means understanding the musical languages to which they are accustomed. One of the things I have most enjoyed is writing musical 'offertories' that are performed at all five services on a Sunday. Three or four minutes of newly composed music reaches thousands of people during a typical Sunday and many people say how important the music is to them. To hear a new piece presented at five services is a real privilege. It helps me to gauge how the music is received by different groups and gives me a sense of unity with the entire church congregation.

If other churches wanted to consider employing a composer, I would offer the following comments:

- It helps to hire someone whose personality, theology and work you already know and appreciate. Talent is important, but a church also needs artists who have a love for the people they serve and the humility to be transparent in what they do.

- A vision of this kind needs to be a shared enterprise. Church leaders and congregation alike need to want new music. UPC is full of educated, intellectually awake people who want to invest in new music because they have identified it as a necessity rather than a luxury. For people at UPC, this is a ministry that feeds and informs in ways that nothing else can.

It was something of an act of faith for the congregation of UPC to take the first steps towards investing in music in this way. They have reaped more benefit than they ever imagined would be possible through hearing the gospel presented in new ways.

Case study 3. Katherine Freeze conducts one of her compositions at UPC, Seattle, October 2000 (photo: Stanley Allen).

4. Storytelling – Raiders of the Lost Art

Anthony Nanson

The art of live storytelling, having almost died out in Britain except in very remote areas, has been in revival since the 1980s. There are now storytelling clubs throughout the country, weekend festivals devoted to storytelling, and an increasing number of performers trying to earn a living by telling stories in pubs, schools, arts centres – anywhere they can find an audience. Interest in storytelling is now reaching the churches, thanks in large measure to The Telling Place initiative, a partnership of the Northumbria Community and the Bible Society, started in 1998. Anthony Nanson is a freelance storyteller, writer and editor. He teaches a course in storytelling at the University of Bath, is the founder of the Bath Storytelling Circle and is the Editor of Artyfact, the magazine of the Arts Centre Group.

The entire tent was packed and an audience of all ages and backgrounds sat transfixed by the words of Mark's Gospel brought to life by a team of ten storytellers. This three-hour epic, performed in the *Telling Place* tent, was for many one of the highlights of *Greenbelt 2000*, the Christian arts festival. Men, women and children were challenged as some of the earliest Christians had been, by encountering Christ through dramatic, passionate, life-changing story.

Simon Airey, a minister who routinely uses storytelling in his work, tells of the intense reactions that are sometimes provoked when Christian themes are brought to life through storytelling. Some people have been deeply moved by stories that help make sense of a lifetime struggling with God. Others have walked out of a story about the Babylonian exile because it conveys so graphically the suffering of the Israelites.

Storytelling has much to offer the life and mission of the church, especially in our present society in which popular culture is dominated by electronic entertainment. Audiences have no real input into the making of a TV programme or movie and no real interaction with the people or characters on the screen. In contrast, storytelling involves real-life, real-time communication between storyteller and listener. The listener's reactions influence the way the stories are told and even which stories are chosen. This provokes a sense of fellowship among the audience, which usually stimulates conversation afterwards. In many storytelling contexts, such as club sessions and ceilidhs (this is an informal evening of stories and music), the floor is open for anyone to contribute a story – there is no fixed boundary between performer and audience.

Appreciating a story requires active listening. Individuals can gain a great boost in self-confidence through having an audience listen to them telling a story. And in a safe context, such as one might expect in a church community, storytelling can be a means for profound sharing of experiences and insights. It also has more specialized applications in education and therapy.

Case study 4. Bobby Baker: 'The Woman who Mistook Her Mouth for a Pocket', A performance at St Luke's Church, Islington (London) as part of the 'Art in Sacred Spaces' project, May 2000 (photo: Andrew Whittuck).

The Christian tradition is already full of stories: Bible stories, stories of saints and missionaries from past and present, the anecdotes with which ministers pepper their sermons, and traditional stories about biblical characters (which may have little basis in history but have value through the truth they tell of faith). There is also a rich Jewish tradition of midrashic stories that comment on Scripture. And, of course, Jesus himself used stories as a primary method of teaching.

Storytelling skills can enliven all this material. In particular they can breathe life into Bible stories so familiar that they may make almost no impact at all when we hear them read from the lectern. There are two main storytelling techniques for recounting biblical stories. The first involves re-telling a story in the teller's own words. The second entails learning the biblical text by heart and telling it more or less verbatim. This is how the Gospel of Mark was told to that tent-full of people at Greenbelt, using the text of the *Contemporary English Version* of the Bible.

Some churches have already begun to experiment with replacing lectern-based Bible readings in worship with verbatim text telling. On occasion, a longer Bible story (perhaps told by more than one person) can be effective in place of both reading and sermon. The challenge is to trust the power of these stories of faith and to trust people's ability to receive wisdom from them, without being prescriptive about what they should mean. When this process works well, it can bring fresh insight to familiar texts. The people who gathered at Greenbelt to hear three hours of Mark's Gospel came away exhilarated from hearing the story of Christ as they had never heard it before.

Most people already have some instinct about how to tell a story, but the development of skills and confidence can benefit from expert help. Hearing good professional storytelling or attending a storytelling workshop are ideal starting points. The Society for Storytelling is one good source of information in Britain and can put you in touch with clubs and storytellers in your region.

However, biblical material tends to be conspicuously absent from secular events. This is where *The Telling Place* steps into the breach. Its main objective is to help the church and wider culture rediscover the power of storytelling – particularly biblical storytelling. *The Telling Place* runs intensive training courses at its headquarters in Northumbria, offers one-day workshops around the country, and will help churches set up a local storytelling group (either to focus on biblical stories or as an open group for all kinds of stories) or put on a ceilidh in someone's home.

The Telling Place has had a prominent presence at festivals such as *Greenbelt* since 1998 and also runs 'Gatherings' as part of its strategy to build up a network of Christian storytellers. It maintains links with the

Network of Biblical Storytellers in the United States, and also with the secular storytelling scene in Britain. Angela Knowles, the main driving force behind *The Telling Place*, has been a professional storyteller since 1989. She has roots in the mainstream storytelling world and was apprenticed to the legendary Scottish storyteller, Duncan Williamson. Acknowledging that much of the best expertise lies outside the church, she involves highly skilled performers from inside and outside the church in the activities of *The Telling Place* and is keen that biblical storytelling in Britain should not become isolated from the larger scene. After all, it is our stories that invite communication and understanding across boundaries of time, culture, and perspective.

Notes

1. The Society for Storytelling publishes a newsletter, *Storylines*, and other publications, and distributes the *Storytelling Diary*, a quarterly listing of performances, club sessions, festivals, and workshops throughout Britain. Contact: PO Box 2344, Reading RG6 7FG; +44 (118) 935 1381; http://www.sfs.org.uk. The *Storytelling Diary* is available directly from Roy Dyson, 70 Church Lane, Underwood, Nottingham NG16 5FS; +44 (1773) 781007; e-mail: roydyson@ntlworld.com. Another British storytelling magazine is Facts & Fiction, from Pete Castle, 190 Burton Road, Derby DE1 1TQ; +44 (1332) 346339; e-mail: steelcarpet@lineone.net

2. For *The Telling Place*, contact Susie Minto, *The Telling Place*, Hetton Hall, Chatton, Alnwick NE66 5SD; +44 (1289) 388477; e-mail: thetellingplace@bigfoot.com

3. The *Network of Biblical Storytellers* can be contacted at +1 (937) 278 5127; e-mail: nobsint@nobs.org; www.nobs.org. The main secular organization in the United States is the National Storytelling Association, which publishes Storytelling Magazine. Contact: PO Box 309, Jonesborough, TN 37659, USA; +1 (423) 753 2171.

Acknowledgement: Thanks to the staff of *The Telling Place* and to Simon Airey for their helpful comments.

5. Faith, Justice and Creativity

Rod Pattenden

Rod Pattenden is the Minister of Paddington Uniting Church in Sydney, Australia. As an artist himself, he has an active interest in the relationship between creativity and faith. He has written and lectured widely on art and faith in Australia, the USA and the UK, and is Co-ordinator of the Institute for Theology and the Arts. Eight years ago, with the support of the congregation at Paddington, he embarked on a unique ministry of outreach through the arts in a lively and diverse urban environment.

What would the church be like if it allowed the arts to contribute to every aspect of its life? How might the arts affect faith if they were allowed to rise above the traditional role of embellishment to incorporate the process of creativity and human inventiveness that is a part of our everyday existence? These are the questions and the challenges that Paddington Uniting church in Sydney Australia has being living with for the last eight years.

The church is situated close to the centre of this large, bustling city in the midst of restaurants, cinemas and galleries, as well as the ever-present realities of urban life such as homelessness and poverty. As both an artist and a minister, I have wondered for some time about how to make the church more aesthetically engaging, more filled with human creativity and more able to reach and nurture people in the midst of glaring social diversity.

To begin that process I turned to the artists, performers and creative people I knew. For twelve months, our regular services of worship bravely introduced contributions from artists, directors, writers, poets and dancers. These people brought with them ideas and practices that were unexpected, quirky, truthful, exciting, challenging and radically different from what people had come to expect from church. They helped the congregation

Case study 5: One of Australia's premiere jazz ensembles 'Clarion Fracture Zone' performs 'Canticle', a work commissioned by the Paddington Uniting Church based on the biblical love poem *Song of Songs*. This work is now available on CD recording, 1999.

nurture their own imagination, inspiring people to express their faith in new ways. The congregation responded by imagining a new role for the church in the community. People saw that the gospel could bring abundant and expressive life that could be nurtured both inside and outside the heritage-listed stone walls of the church building.

A number of specific projects were developed in the second year that sought to affirm the place of creativity in the life of the congregation. These projects ranged from 'hobby' Sundays to regular services featuring the creative talents of parishioners. People enjoyed themselves and felt that they were able to bring more of their life into the place and act of worship. This, in turn, began to affect perceptions about mission in the community. As people saw new possibilities within the church, they started to see new opportunities outside the church.

One of the key areas of the church's mission has been to provide hospitality to people facing homelessness, and accompanying problems such as substance abuse, in the inner city. The church gave support to a welfare worker who wanted to develop a writing and poetry group. Over twelve months this group met weekly, gradually developing interest through reading the folk tradition of Australian stories and poetry. Over time, members of the group began to write down their own stories in poetic form. Soon there was enough good material for the group to consider publication.

With a grant from the church's welfare agency, a book that highlighted the comic and tragic stories of these women and men was published with illustrations by our newly developed art class. There was much joy when the book was launched by one of Australia's more significant media figures who read a selection of contributions from the writers. This project succeeded in giving a voice to the voiceless using the strategies provided by the arts. The book was made available in local bookstores and succeeded in returning a small amount of money from sales to each contributor.

The awareness that all human beings are creative and have a story to tell is something that has inspired members of the congregation to maintain that value for themselves. As a result of experimentation with the arts, the church rewrote its mission statement around the three words: *faith, justice and creativity*. A vision of the gospel has emerged that sees creativity as a central mark of the freedom that Christ gives all people, irrespective of their situation in life.

Given the success of early projects, the arts began to have a more central role in the planning and development of the church's property resources and, over time, more facilities have been made available. Given the scarcity of good rehearsal and performance facilities in the locality, the church has been able to develop a series of partnerships with outside organizations and groups. This helps to sustain the building that in turn nurtures the people who use it. This has become an important source of income and has enabled us to improve facilities, lighting and sound over the last five years.

The increased activity has enabled us to employ a part time Arts Officer who oversees these developments under the umbrella identity of 'Eastside

Arts'. Under this banner, the church sponsors a diverse range of regular concerts (from à capella and jazz to classical music), exhibitions and workshops. One of the more recent creative outcomes that has been inspired by these partnerships is the commissioning of a number of art works and an extended jazz poem around the theme of the Song of Songs in the Old Testament. This has now been released as a CD recording.

Listing achievements is always encouraging, but there have also been failures along the way. We have entertained partnerships that were not successful and have been used by people wanting only to further their own career. We have learned that risk is part and parcel of the adventure of embracing the arts. Some of our findings at Paddington can be summarized as follows.

1. Artists have taught us that life is messy, creative and full of possibilities. We now recognize that artistic skills like improvisation and creativity enable us to face the future with courage to experiment (and sometimes fail) along the way.

2. As a community, we value inspiration, truthfulness and a sense of relevance. A truthful connection to real issues can be aided and sustained by having ears to hear and eyes to see. The arts help us to do this more effectively.

3. The arts help to translate faith into action when we encounter the harsher sides of contemporary life. Heightening our awareness of issues like justice, the arts allow creativity and hope to influence the future. This makes the gospel a matter of public concern and celebration.

The arts have helped our community break down the false divide between the inside and the outside, and between sacred and secular, in a way that has breathed new life and relevance into our sense of identity and mission.

6. Engaging with Contemporary Culture through Contemporary Art

Julia Porter Price, Anne Mullins and Paul Lowe

As part of London's celebrations for the new millennium, a group of Anglican clergy took the bold step of applying for Millennium Commission funding in order to commission a number of works from major secular artists to be displayed in 'sacred spaces'. The money was secured and the resulting works were to be displayed in a series of churches, synagogues and a mosque in London. The high profiles (and controversial reputations) of a number of the artists who took part ensured that the project hit the headlines on more than one occasion, forcing the churches and artists involved to articulate their motivations to the wider world. Although some of the media reaction was critical, much was sympathetic and a follow-up project is now being planned.

People say they don't understand what contemporary art is about;
I've never understood what religion is about ...
(Artist in conversation at the Round Chapel, Clapton)

'Art in Sacred Spaces' started as a conversation around a kitchen table among a group of Anglicans interested in contemporary art. At the time, money was being made available through the Millennium Commission for all kinds of projects. Many involved art, but few involved religion. Here was an opportunity to initiate a project that would:

- challenge assumptions about contemporary art;
- challenge assumptions about religion;

- open up sacred spaces to new audiences;

- take contemporary art to new audiences;

- create dialogue between artists, art audiences and faith communities.

Getting going

The original plan was to commission artists to create an art trail in 15 churches in East London (Islington, Hackney and Tower Hamlets) on the themes of creation, redemption and liberation. With an award of £25,000 from the Millennium Festival Fund, a steering group, drawn from people in Anglican churches with experience of the visual arts, appointed Anne Mullins, a freelance arts consultant, as Project Manager in March 1999. The steering group was authorized in April 1999 to form a company limited by guarantee to manage the project on behalf of the London Diocese (Stepney Area). The company, St.Art 2000, gained charitable status in April 2000.

It became clear that funding would be insufficient to commission 15 new works, as envisaged in the ambitious original proposal. The number was reduced to 12 and the concept of 'commission' extended to include work never previously shown in sacred spaces. A total of £56,500 was raised from a mix of trusts, local authority grants and public funds; a further £42,000 came from sponsorship in kind. Seven new works were finally commissioned.

Developing the idea

Venues housing different worshipping communities were selected to create a trail through Islington, Hackney and Tower Hamlets; criteria included architectural/geographical prominence and access by public transport, with priority given to venues with experience of working with artists. Each had the option to veto who or what would be displayed. Opening hours were suggested to the venues and standardized as far as possible, subject to weddings, funerals, religious festivals etc. A three-week period was thought to be manageable. In response to growing concern about staffing the exhibition, a volunteer co-ordinator was brought in to help organize invigilation.

One of the most exciting elements of the project was the potential for artists to work with congregations or groups within the community to explore the spiritual themes of creation, redemption and liberation in new ways. To encourage this interaction, an Artist's Brief was developed and circulated in June 1999.

We are looking for artists excited by the opportunity to:

- produce a site-specific work for a church/place of worship in East London (Islington, Hackney, Tower Hamlets)

- engage with spiritual themes: creation, redemption, liberation

- enter into dialogue with local/worshipping communities

- access non-art audiences (as well as art audiences)

Proposals are welcomed from artists of faith/no faith, new/established, all ages & all cultures. We are particularly keen to receive proposals from new artists, artists of colour, artists working with disability. Experience of working with school groups could be useful. East London connections are an advantage.

As things turned out, not all the artists selected were able to work in this way, due to lack of time. Those who did found the process of working with worshipping communities to be the most valuable part of the project.

The reality of working in a large city inevitably introduced factors that couldn't be foreseen. Artist Keith Khan, who masterminded the Dome's opening ceremony as production designer, suffered a brutal racist attack shortly before undertaking his project. On crutches and in plaster, he involved the multi-cultural church community with whom he was working in creating a piece about racial violence.

Tracey Emin is notorious for *Everyone I've Ever Slept With* (an embroidered tent) and *My Bed* (the piece shortlisted for the Turner Prize which features condoms and soiled sheets). For 'Art in Sacred Spaces', Emin exchanged shock tactics for something much more innocent. She chose to work with children at a local church school to produce a patchwork quilt called *Tell Me Something Beautiful*.

Unusually in the art world, 'Art in Sacred Spaces' put artists who are extremely well known (Tracey Emin, Rachel Whiteread, Mark Wallinger and Damien Hirst) alongside new and emerging artists. Art critic Celia Lyttelton commented: 'Not all the artists involved are ardent worshippers, and their

Case study 6. 'Defying Dog' by David Cotterrell, an interactive video piece, exploring the changing role of churches in a multimedia age, commissioned for 'Art in Sacred Spaces' and installed at The Round Church, Hackney, London, May 2000 (copyright David Cotterrell).

commissions were hardly lucrative, but they have entered into the spirit of the project' (Celia Lyttelton, Associated Newspapers, May 31, 2000).

Reactions

The decision to include Tracey Emin and Damien Hirst was taken after much discussion, and it was felt that this needed careful handling. It was decided to appoint a freelance press officer to handle marketing and publicity for the project from January 2000. The media attention was immediate. The majority of the coverage sough to sensationalize the work of such controversial secular artists being shown in churches. There were also several thoughtful reports and reviews which stimulated discussion about the relationship between art and religion.

The opening event at St Luke, West Holloway, on 21 May 2000, drew a healthy audience comprising ordinary church-goers, art-lovers and the press. For many of these people attending a church service was an extremely unusual experience. A performance by Bobby Baker, a member of the congregation, was incorporated into the service as a 'sermon' on sin. Despite being unfamiliar territory for many, this was a relaxed occasion.

Children sat on the floor in the aisle to see better and the majority stayed to talk over coffee and wine after the service.

Around 5,000 people saw the exhibition during its three-week period.

Thinking about it

There have been tensions working between cultures: the culture of the (Anglican) church and the culture of the art world, the culture of artists and the culture of different faith communities. There have also been practical issues for artists and faith communities about working with sacred spaces. For artists, accustomed to exhibiting mostly in galleries, lighting could not be controlled, security was limited, colour schemes and other furnishings were fixed and in some cases there was not even any wall space.

It is amazing that the project happened at all, given the limited resources, shoestring budget and experimental nature of the work. As an arts outreach project, it worked well. As an outreach project on the part of the faith communities, it is harder to assess its impact. While the project was not evangelistic in purpose, doors were opened and conversations begun. Good relationships have been established, particularly across faith communities. The enterprise has generated wide interest and a number of suggestions for developing dialogue between artists and faith communities have emerged: a register of loans, technical advice for artists working in sacred spaces, and a fund to commission permanent work for sacred spaces. A five-year plan is now being developed and office space sought to provide a base for the work.

7. Meeting the Neighbours:
community arts and youth mission at Romsey Mill

Andrew Rumsey

Romsey Mill is a youth and community centre in Romsey Town, Cambridge. It is a charitable organization that was set up by local churches in 1980 to serve the needs of the local community, which it does through numerous staff and volunteers. Their work especially supports young families and young people who face social exclusion.

Engaging in local mission today can be a scary business – and not just for the Christians. One of the hardest aspects of bridging the gap between church and non-church worlds is the mutual suspicion and fear that each has of the other. As churches become increasingly sealed off from the communities in which they are set, outreach can easily become *Star Trek*-style excursions from the mother ship into alien territory, with all the awkwardness and bad acting that involves. Likewise, having assimilated the media portrayal of believers as either amusing relics or sinister fanatics, non-church individuals and institutions may well hide behind the couch when the Christians come calling.

In such a climate the onus is on the church to express the gospel in ways that people can understand, so that, over time, relationships of trust can be established that allow authentic exchange. Community arts can and should play a key role here – not as a sort of 'false beard' to disguise the Christian message, but as a genuine and sensitive means of engagement. *Community* art is distinctive in that it is not so much art *for* a particular group as art *with* a particular group. It involves working across cultural and social boundaries with the express purpose of building relationships.

The place of artistic expression has always been central to outreach for Romsey Mill, beginning with what became known as 'The Romsey Mill

Roadshow'. In the 1980s the centre purchased some second-hand record decks and lighting boxes and developed a portable event loosely based on the then popular BBC Radio 1 Roadshow. Through music, games and drama, young people were introduced to issues of faith in a format they already recognized – making it possible for them to encounter the gospel without being distracted by an unfamiliar medium.

One of the challenges faced by this kind of outreach is the constant need to adapt to an ever-changing youth scene (Radio Roadshows are quickly outdated). Whatever the format, though, we found that two-way *involvement* and *communication* were the key.

Romsey Mill's work in the community flourished, in part at least, because of this. It sought to pay genuine attention to those it served and was there in the community (and still is) for the long haul.

Involvement meant real and committed engagement with the community. *Communication* meant listening as well as speaking; enabling the stranger's voice to be heard so that *who they were* could intersect in authentic ways with *who God is*. Art was central to this task; allowing the encounter to happen in natural, neutral cultural territory while giving colour and definition to often half-formed questions of identity and

Case study 7. A warm-up session for a group of teenagers, 'Inside out' project, Kettle's Yard, Cambridge, 1990 (photo: Sarah Derrick).

belonging. By encouraging people to think about who and where they were, this opened up new possibilities as to what they could become.

In its work with young people, the Romsey Mill has embraced this approach in a variety of ways, from allowing space within the centre for murals by local graffiti artists to providing equipment and time for aspiring DJs to practice their skills. Notably, it has also run a photography project for young women in association with Cambridge City Council that culminated in a fascinating exhibition of pictures relating to their locality.

One of the most popular services the team at Romsey Mill developed was the running of drama workshops. None of the staff were formally trained in performing arts, but simply liked drama and saw that this was a natural and enjoyable way for the young people to engage with all kinds of issues and ideas. A simple and repeatable format was developed that built up from drama exercises and *Whose Line is it Anyway?* games to a point where the group produced and/or performed a piece of their own. The sessions (which could work with groups of four to forty in number) were then offered to local schools and community groups, many of whom were only too glad to have local involvement and assistance. These workshops could be adapted and themed according to the age of the participants and the purpose of the session. The results were usually hilarious and often remarkably fruitful.

8. Creative Writing and Pastoral Care

Andrew Rumsey

Andrew Rumsey is an ordained priest in the Church of England. Previously he worked for the ground-breaking Christian community centre, Romsey Mill, and in arts marketing for Cambridge City Council. Andrew is involved in the project 'Theology Through the Arts', for whom he contributed a chapter to Beholding the Glory *(DLT). He has also published a booklet of poems,* Homing In *(Solway), and performs his songs and poems in numerous church halls, pubs and clubs. More recently he has begun running workshops in creative writing as an experiment in pastoral care.*

Word-play

Going around, in the time-honoured fashion, the group nervously introduced themselves and their experience of 'this sort of thing'. It wasn't a promising start. A few enjoyed reading a bit, a very few liked poetry and even fewer had ever attempted writing any. By the end of the session, a young woman locked up with emotional difficulties had written a long, intensely moving prayer; one man from the local 'problem' housing estate delivered a ready-to-sing hymn and another had produced a short story relating long-suppressed family traumas. Remarkable. It was this experience, at a creative writing workshop led by my mother, that prompted me some twenty years later to begin exploring the power of words in pastoral care.

In particular it has been this 'workshop' model that I have found most fruitful in encouraging churches to discover creative writing. This has worked in many different ways: as an optional session at a church weekend away, a retreat day, or even as the basis for a regular fellowship group. The equipment needed is minimal: a comfortable room to use, a few examples of good creative writing and a dozen pads and pencils.

The format has proved surprisingly adaptive, from light-hearted sessions composing excruciating limericks to more pastorally-focused times of preparing psalms and prayers together. The one often leads naturally to the other; the best workshops being those with both hilarity and depth.

Why words?

Why should writing be so rewarding? 'Some words', wrote W. S. Gilbert, ' teem with hidden meaning.' In poem, lyric, novel or play, words are used creatively to reveal what is usually hidden, expressing what we thought was there but perhaps could not articulate. A line from a song or script can make us catch our breath in shock, cringe with embarrassment, or leave us helpless with laughter. Words used well (whether in a Shakespeare sonnet or a Robbie Williams song) resonate with our experience, share our situation, and move us on. Words are advocates, counsellors.

Creative writing, or 'painting with words', has a special capacity to reveal or express truth about life and therefore holds special pastoral value. Christians should, after all, be at home with the power of words; consider for a moment the opening of St John's Gospel:

> In the beginning was the Word,
> and the Word was with God,
> and the Word was God.

John goes on to describe this 'Word' having been present in the very act of creation and finally taking our flesh as the man Jesus. Christ is the creative Word, present with us by the Holy Spirit – described by John as our advocate and counsellor. This dynamic understanding of the presence of God allows us to speak of the Bible as 'the word of God' because, through words, it reveals and articulates God in Christ.

Words, then, are a gift of God in creation, and there is something about written words (whether our own or those of someone else) which is especially releasing and helpful. Spilling your mixed-up feelings, fears or prayers on to paper 'gets them out', rearranging them on the page is an act of hope and healing.

I am always taken aback by how fruitful creative writing workshops are. It is very often the people I expect to be the least forthcoming (the inexperienced, perhaps, or the tongue-tied) who produce the most moving and interesting work.

Case study 8. A creative writing session fires imagination as part of David Cotterrell's work at Rushmore Primary School in Clapton, Hackney for 'Art in Sacred Spaces', May 2000 (photo: David Cotterrell).

Words of advice

I have found the following principles helpful for running creative writing workshops in a church context.

- *Skill.* People attending the session do not need to be well-read or experienced in writing. The leader needs to have enough skill and familiarity with literature to choose and share examples from appropriate writers, and the ability to lead people through from simple ideas to more complex ones (starting with basic word games, for example, and encouraging people on as they gain confidence).

- *Sensitivity.* Creative writing can be a very personal exercise (especially if what we have written is shared with others). The leader/facilitator of the session must be sensitive to people's vulnerability and pastorally mature enough to handle painful or difficult issues that may arise.

- *Confidentiality.* Even light-hearted sessions work better when members agree that no material shared in the group should be used afterwards (in services, for example) without the author's permission. A secure environment encourages free expression.

- *Balance.* The most helpful sessions are those that allow plenty of room for hilarity and enjoyment, permitting the 'deep stuff' to be expressed naturally without being levered out.

- *Timing.* It is hard to get very far in less than two hours. Regular short meetings or one longer session (e.g. a day) can work equally well. Regular breaks (for body and mind) are important for sessions lasting more than a couple of hours.

- *Numbers.* An ideal number is between 8 and 20 people.

A picture can, we are told, speak a thousand words. Equally, a few words, carefully chosen, can paint a thousand pictures.

9. Choreography – Inspiration and Perspiration: the creative process from a Christian perspective

Sara Savage

Sara Savage is trained as a professional dancer (ballet and contemporary techniques) and a social psychologist. She is currently Senior Research Associate with the Psychology and Christianity Project at Cambridge University, and lectures in psychology, sociology and research methods in the Cambridge Theological Federation. Prior to her academic career, Sara danced full-time for 12 years with a Christian dance company. She now dances with and directs the dance group Icon and has a particular interest in the psychological aspects of how movement and dance relate to faith.

Choreography: inspiration

Inspiration is, by definition, difficult to describe. If we could conjure up creativity at will, it is likely that the arts would cease to have the capacity to inspire. There remains an element of mystery in the process. In Christian circles, the possibility of God's activity within the creative process further complicates any attempt to describe how a Christian artist is inspired to paint, compose or choreograph.

Only in looking back over years of experience can I describe what the creative process of choreography seems to be like. With the benefit of hindsight, I compare the choreographic process to the rules of *haiku*, a Japanese form of poetry. I don't use these rules to make a dance 'happen', but in retrospect, I observe that the elements are often present.

Haiku poems are very short, containing only 17 syllables in three lines. This is considered to be the duration of a moment of *satori* – flash of inspirational insight or poetic shock. Haiku seeks to unfold truth about the world by focusing on a microcosmic, concrete reality – a reference to nature, or a moment in time. The poems are not stories, but observations, inviting the reader to participate with the senses and imagination in the scene that first ignited the moment of *satori* conveyed.[33]

Not unlike the poetic shock that ignites a haiku, a dance with a spiritual message 'happens' upon me. I cannot conjure one up, yet I need to be receptive to the ever-present possibility of inspiration. Often it comes in response to hearing a piece of music, even one or two notes. Those notes inscribe themselves upon me; they continue to work on my emotions until I begin to 'unearth' the dance suggested by the music. I often don't know what the dance is about at first; I only know the strong feeling I have experienced.

I spend time in God's presence to let that feeling unfold. This is where the collaborative work happens; I invite the Holy Spirit to be involved. I gradually become aware of the theme or direction the dance may go in. I imagine various movements. I draw upon twelve years of dance training in ballet and contemporary dance to provide a vocabulary for the feelings and thoughts that are emerging. Other media may become part of the dance as well: drama, readings, visual images, sound effects, symbolic objects, and sets. When I am *surprised* by the way ideas begin to gel, I feel I might be on the right track.

Like haiku, most of my dances are 'small'. Often performed in church, they do not take up much space or time. More importantly, the narrative of the dance is circumscribed. I do not attempt to tackle a theme like redemption, or the history of Israel's kings. Instead, dances centre on a concrete moment in time and space: Mary pondering the words spoken to her by the angel about Jesus; the anguished prayer of a Polish prisoner in concentration camp; the disciples taking down the body of Christ from the cross.

The internal comparison happens on many levels. There is often some struggle or transition in my own life that bears some resemblance to the theme of the dance. However, the dance is not about me; rather, I use my experience as a microcosm that points towards a macrocosm beyond my own experience.

Like a haiku, dance is ultimately about an emotional response to insight. This does not mean it is devoid of intellectual content. Emotions have a strong cognitive component. They arise from a certain way of perceiving and making sense of the world. Emotion also tends to be in motion – unfolding,

---

33   Rules of Haiku adapted from H G Henderson, *Haiku in English* (Tokyo: Charles E. Tuttle Co., 1967).

and transmuting. True to this quality of emotion, my dances bear a kind of narrative structure, either abstract or concrete. Change is at the core of physical movement, and the heart of dance. As a Christian choreographer, I focus on the kind of change that is central to the Christian life, the kinds of change involved in prayer, repentance, hope, faith or despair. My aim is that the dances will be tiny windows through which we can glimpse something of the mystery of the incarnate Christ at work in human experience.

Choreography: perspiration

A case study of a dance in progress

- *Dance:* 'The Deposition'
- *Music:* 'Praise to the Immortality of Jesus' (*Louange à l'Immortalité de Jésus*) from the *Quartet for the End of Time* by Olivier Messaien

In 1940, Olivier Messaien wrote his *Quartet for the End of Time* in a concentration camp, and performed it in the freezing, harrowing conditions of the prison. The melody of the section Praise to the Immortality of Jesus progresses unrelentingly upwards; nothing on earth can violate the sublime eternity of God and the immortality of Christ, not even the unendurable conditions that gave birth to the composition. The music reaches beyond time, beyond suffering and pain to eternity and immortality.

I first heard this music in a theology lecture given by Jeremy Begbie. I felt compelled to find out what the music was saying to me, and listened to it again and again. Many months later, through a deep personal loss and my grieving in prayer, the feelings the music had touched began to make sense. But the dance was not to be about my loss, but the loss the disciples felt as they had the horrific task of taking down the body of Christ from the cross. Their story took over. 'The Deposition' (the taking down of the body of Christ from the cross) began to evolve.

I asked three trained dancers (from Icon Dance Company), and Revd John Naude, a wheelchair athlete, to be involved in the dance; I had danced with John before and knew of his amazing ability for expressive movement and how he uses the wheelchair in exciting and surprising ways to extend the choreographic possibilities. The four dancers moving together spoke profoundly of the abilities within disabilities that are part of all our lives. This functioned like an internal comparison in a haiku poem: ability within disability, life within death. This core meaning of the dance hung upon the tension between music and movement. In contrast to the timelessness of

Case study 9. Dress rehearsal for 'The Deposition' with dancers from Icon Dance Company, September 2000 (copyright Sara Savage).

Messaien's music, the dance moves into time, and into suffering and pain, focusing on the finite, dead body of Christ. This tension (between music and movement) became the scaffold for the whole dance.

I hoped to remain faithful to that moment of satori, and often returned to it in prayer. Like a haiku, our dance focused on a tiny segment of the passion narrative, but within this a whole world of meaning began to unfold.

The choreography helped to crystallize a paper I was writing on the way dance can help us to recapture the humanness of Christ through recapturing our own. The paper was to become a chapter in a larger book on the arts and incarnation[34] and so it was decided that the dance would be performed as part of the launch for the book. With this commission, serious work started.

The dancers and I met for two hours most Monday evenings for over six months. These rehearsals involved much perspiration; the original inspiration seemed remote. I often had little idea of how the movements should proceed, but felt they were to be limited to four or five themes: grief (curling in a ball and rocking), need (reaching vertically upwards), revulsion (turning away), depression (gravity bound falls) and despair (reckless acts of throwing oneself). I gave these themes to the dancers and asked them to improvise to the music. Their movements produced many ideas, and we settled on a movement motif choreographed by Alison Eve incorporating the themes. I added variations and inversions of the lines and energy dynamics as the dance progressed.

However, I decided to respond to the character of Messaien's music by echoing his restraint, deliberately selecting a minimal range of movements from the wider choreographic 'palette'.

At every stage, we returned to prayer. My job as the choreographer was sometimes merely to say, 'Yes, that's it', or 'No, that doesn't work'. Sometimes I would choreograph whole sections myself. At other times, I would say to the others, 'I don't know what to do here.' We worked together. Our disagreements were disciplined by the fact that all of us wanted to 'glimpse' the meaning of Christ's passion through what we were doing.

The dance required a large set, and I worked with an artist on its construction. Our ideas led to a black scaffolding triptych, upon which would hang an larger than life abstract fabric sculpture of the torn body of Christ made from the white silk of a WW2 parachute. It is the task of the dancers to take down this torn body. The cold, strong lighting effects suggested prison conditions; barbed wire ran along the top of the 20-foot high triptych, a snarl of wire hinting at a crown of thorns. The only moment

---

34 Jeremy Begbie, ed., *Beholding the Glory: Incarnation Through the Arts* (Grand Rapids: Baker, 2000).

of colour in this monochrome setting was the flash of blinding red light that showed momentarily through the black, like a shock of pain that pierces through numbness. Towards the end of the dance, as the mourning rites conclude, the body is unfurled into the air, opening like wings and covering the dancers in a cloud of white. With this glimpse of resurrection, the dancers wrap up and carry out the body, as the music rises to the highest register.

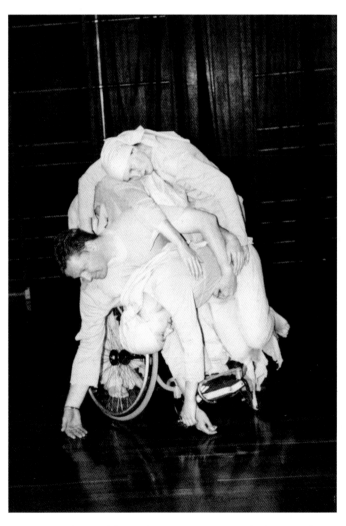

Case study 9. Dress rehearsal for 'The Deposition' with dancers from Icon Dance Company, September 2000 (copyright Sara Savage).

10. Dealing with a Wired World: technology and the church

Ben Witherington III

Ben Witherington is Professor of New Testament at Asbury Theological Seminary in Wilmore, Kentucky. He is also a fellow of Robinson College, Cambridge and an adjunct member of St Mary's College, University of St Andrews. He is well-known for his numerous commentaries and books in New Testament and Christian origins, such as the award-winning The Jesus Quest *(Paternoster: Carlisle, 1995) (*Christianity Today *Book of the year, 1995) and* The Paul Quest *(IVP: Leicester, 1998). He has been developing a particular interest in the role of technology for Christian education and the church.*

It stands to reason that in an information age words must be important, and none more so than the Word. But strangely enough, those most responsible for communicating the Word have often been slow to get on the information super-highway. Like an Amish buggy on Interstate 40, some assume that as long as we are on the right road, we will eventually get there. But technology just doesn't work like that and if we don't travel with the rest of the traffic, we may lose our way altogether.

There is no virtue in adopting an electronically-challenged attitude to technology. It is also futile to complain about the litter along the way as if that were an excuse for not travelling at all.

Technology is already allowing people to communicate in ways that are changing our world. Will Christians take a lead in this process, or avoid it? And what are the implications of either option for a church which professes to be solidly committed to the Word?

Who would ever have imagined that modems, faxes and e-mail would revive the lost art of letter writing? Who would ever have predicted that the electronic era would bring back the literary arts or make writing easier? In the electronic age prose, poetry, music, painting all have become easier to produce, even mass produce. Who would have predicted that in an electronic culture Americans would spend more on books than on any other kind of entertainment?

John Perry Barlow said that the invention of electronics would have more impact on our culture than the invention of fire. Perhaps that is already true. This should be good news for the Good News because wires and lines and modems and faxes and e-mails and the rest are tools for conveying words – so they may as well convey the Word. Yet the church sometimes seems to be the least technologically literate organization on earth. What does it mean for the church to get wired, hear the hum, see the vision, capture the image?

I have no doubt that we will have to recontextualize our ministries of education. The old philosophy – 'if we build it they will come' – has only limited usefulness in the electronic age. Communication by extension, whether in person or by downlink or in some virtual form, is happening and will continue to happen. The question is whether the church will take advantage of it. Will we be able to harness its obvious promise while avoiding drawbacks, such as the lack of personal interaction?

At Asbury Seminary I can now present lectures in the TV studio. This means that I can reach more students than can fit in a classroom, without having to give the lecture twice. By simultaneous broadcast, I can still take questions and I end up with more time for tutorials, electives, writing projects, and other tasks of ministry. In the information age we may not need a thousand repetitions of the same lecture or sermon, we may only need one or two good ones per year with excellent satellite hookups and downlinks.

Technology not only allows us to reach more people, it allows us to reach them more effectively. I now use the following in addition to traditional teaching material:

1. *Video clips from movies* – from *Ben Hur* to *Bladerunner*, AD to Apocalypse Now, movies can inform, challenge and stimulate. (NB While one can do this for educational purposes, it is not wise to try to market the video tapes; the permissions are generally either expensive or not yet forthcoming.) Why are movie clips an important tool? Because we live in an age of predominantly visual learners – the TV-, movie-, computer screen-, Gameboy-generation.

2. *Powerpoint presentations.* I can either do these as overheads to reinforce main points, or else display them directly from my laptop by plugging it

Case study 10. *Cyberspace*, a digital image, by Jonathan Kearney.

into a data projector. Anything on my laptop can be put up on the screen for all to see, including maps, art pictures, text fragments and much more.

3. *Music.* Although we live in a visual age it also has a dominant aural subculture based in the music industry. Music of all kinds is more popular than ever. Jesus with jazz, Paul with rock pizzazz or Pentecost with Prokofiev – all can lend something more than word and image alone.

The goal is that the message will be memorable, not trivialized, and that the hearer will experience total saturation learning through using eye and ear, mind and heart. If 'the heart has reasons that the mind knows not of', if 'the Spirit prays through us with sighs too deep for words', it will not be enough to offer *logos* if we do not also offer *pathos*. It requires that we use the whole spectrum of learning tools if we are to reach the whole person with the whole gospel, taking every thought and feeling captive for Christ.

And what of the Internet – already wired to deliver ideas through word, image and sound?

In some ways Protestants are well behind Catholics in these matters. Roman Catholics are sending missionaries into cyberspace, they have their own home pages on the Internet, believers can make their confession while surfing the net or they can download items from a Catholic library of 30,000 documents. There are forums and chat rooms, and people are talking and talking and talking to them. It is no longer enough to advertise on the Internet and have a homepage. Interaction is required. Believe it or not, even the Amish are doing this! The Amish have their own homepage called 'Ask the Amish'.

There is a wonderful TV commercial that highlights the promise of the information age. It shows, among others, a speech-impaired girl, an old black lady, a young boy and others; it says, 'On the Internet there is no race, no gender, no age, only minds.' This made me wonder if, when Paul said 'In Christ there is no Jew or Gentile, slave or free, no male and female', he envisaged a means of communicating in which appearance or age or race or gender would be laid aside? If it is true that God's face cannot be seen and that he doesn't look on one's outward appearance, then the Internet is surely a place both for God and for God's gospel. Yet there is also a need for caution. A disembodied voice leaves little room to detect irony, sarcasm, plaintiveness or, worse, predation.

Critical thinking about the use of technology is, of course, still in its early stages, not least because there are huge issues about intellectual property and what happens to it when it is made available on line. Publishers have been struggling to come up with formulations that can solve the issues relating to copyright laws. Some artists are concerned about the way an interactive two-dimensional medium will affect the experience of three-dimensional objects. Can incarnational learning or experiencing, which seems to require presence rather than virtual reality, happen through the Net?

We have to ask these questions because refusing the advances of technology makes a powerful (and negative) statement to the wider, wired world. If we are to reach whole people with the whole gospel we may have to be prepared to join the fast lane of the information super-highway.

Section 4

Resources

Section 4. Children's painting workshop led by Ian Davenport, at Dundee Contemporary Arts, 1999 (copyright DCA).

Further Reading

General Resources – artists and events

Arts in Mission Resource Directory (Swindon: British and Foreign Bible
   Society, 1998)

How to Organize an Event (English Tourist Board)

J J Goldblat, *Special Events: Best Practice in Modern Event Management*
   (1997)

S Passingham, *Organizing Local Events* (Directory of Social Change, 1993)

Gerry Robinson, *The Creativity Imperative: Investing in the Arts in the 21st
   Century* (London: Arts Council of England, 2000)

Sheila Rowley and Stephen Woollett, *Entertainment, Events and Exhibitions:
   Bringing Arts to Village Halls* (Cirencester: ACRE 1991)

Phyllida Shaw, ed., *Re-creating Communities: Business, The Arts and Social
   Regeneration* (London: Arts & Business, 1999)

Sue Stayte and David C Watt, *Events from Start to Finish* (Reading: Institute
   of Leisure and Amenity Management, 1998)

Fund Raising

Owen Bevan, Johanna Davis and David Moncrieff, eds., *The Directory of
   Grant Making Trusts* (West Malling: Charities Aid Foundation, republished each year)

Luke Fitzherbert, Dominic Addison an Faisel Rahman, *A Guide to the Major
   Trusts* (London: Directory of Social Change, republished each year)

Susan Forrester and Graeme Manuel, *Arts Funding Guide* (London: The Directory of Social Change[5], 2000)

Arts in Worship

Paul Alexander, *Creativity in Worship* (London: Darton, Longman and Todd, 1990)

Daniel W Hardy and David F Ford, *Jubilate: Theology in Praise* (London: Darton, Longman and Todd, 1984)

Mary Jones, *God's people on the Move: A Manual for Leading Congregations in Dance and Movement* (New South Wales, Australia: Christian Dance Fellowship of Australia, 1988)

Arts-Christian Interface

Diane Apostolos-Cappadona, *Art, Creativity and the Sacred: An Anthology in Religion and Art* (New York: Crossroad, 1984)

Bruce Babington and P W Evans, *Biblical Epics. Sacred Narrative in the Hollywood Cinema* (Manchester University Press/St Martin's Press, 1993)

Stephen Barton, *Invitation to the Bible* (London: SPCK, 1997)

Jeremy Begbie, *Music in God's Purposes* (Edinburgh: Handsel Press, 1989)

—*Theology, Music and Time* (Cambridge: Cambridge University Press, 2000)

—*Voicing Creation's Praise: Towards a Theology of the Arts* (Edinburgh: T. & T. Clark, 1991)

Harold Best, *Music Through the Eyes of Faith* (San Francisco: Harper, 1993)

Hilary Brand and Adrienne Chaplin, *Art and Soul: Signposts for Christians in the Arts* (Carlisle: Solway, 1999; updated edition forthcoming Carlisle: Piquant, 2001)

David Brown and Ann Loades, *The Sense of the Sacramental: Movement and Measure in Art and Music, Place and Time* (London: SPCK, 1995)

Christopher Campling, *The Food of Love: Reflections on Music and Faith* (London: SCM, 1997)

Brian Draper and Kevin Draper, *Refreshing Worship* (Bible Reading Fellowship, 2000)

Tim Dean and David Porter, eds., *Art in Question* (Basingstoke: Marshall Pickering, 1987)

Jane Dillenberger, *Style and Content in Christian Art* (New York: Crossroads, 1986)

David F Ford and Dennis Stamps, eds., *Essentials of Christian Community* (Edinburgh: T & T Clark, 1996)

David F Ford, *The Shape of Living* (London: Fount, 1997)

Nigel Forde, *The Lantern and the Looking-Glass: Literature and Christian Belief* (London: SPCK, 1997)

—*Theatrecraft, Creativity and the Art of Drama* (Wheaton: Shaw, 1990)

Frank Gaebelein, *The Christian, The Arts, and Truth: Regaining the Vision of Greatness* (Portland: Multnomah, 1985)

Nadine Gordimer, *Culture in Another South Africa* (ed. William Campschreur & Joost Divendal; London: Zed Books, 1989)

Robert Jewett, *Saint Paul at the Movies: The Apostle's Dialogue with American Culture* (Louisville: Westminster/John Knox, 1993)

Madeleine L'Engle, *Walking on Water: Reflections on Faith and Art* (New York: Bantam, 1980)

Clive Marsh and Gaye Ortiz, eds., *Explorations in Theology and Film* (Oxford: Blackwell, 1997)

Margaret R Miles, *Image as Insight: Visual Understanding in Western Christianity and Secular Culture* (Boston: Beacon, 1985)

Henri J. M. Nouwen, *The Return of the Prodigal Son: A Story of Homecoming* (London: Darton, Longman & Todd, 1992).

Hans Rookmaaker, *Art Needs No Justification* (Leicester: IVP, 1978)

—*Modern Art and the Death of a Culture* (Leicester: IVP, 1970; 1973[2], re-issued Leicester: Apollos, 1994)

Dorothy Sayers, *The Mind of the Maker* (London: Religious Book Club, 1942[3])

Calvin Seerveld, *Bearing Fresh Olive Leaves* (Carlisle: Piquant, 2000)

—*Rainbows for the Fallen World: Aesthetic Life and Artistic Task* (Toronto: Tuppence Press, 1980)

Francis Schaeffer, *Art and the Bible: Two Essays* (Downers Grove, Ill: Intervarsity, 1973)

Franky Schaeffer, *Addicted to Mediocrity: Twentieth Century Christians and the Arts* (Westchester: Crossway, 1981)

Steve Scott, *Like A House on Fire* (Chicago: Cornerstone Press, 1997)

William David Spencer and Aida Besancon Spencer, eds., *God Through the Looking Glass: Glimpses from the Arts* (Grand Rapids: Baker, 1998 and Carlisle: Paternoster, 1998)

Gene Veith, *The Gift of Art: The Place of the Arts in Scripture* (Downers Grove, Ill: Intervarsity, 1983)

—*State of the Arts: From Bezalel to Mapplethorpe* (Wheaton: Crossway, 1991)

Andrew Walker, *Telling the Story: Gospel, Mission and Culture* (London: SPCK, 1996)

Murray Watts, *Christianity and the Theatre* (Edinburgh: Handsel, 1986)

John Wilson, *One of the Richest Gifts: An Introductory Study of the Arts from a Christian World-view* (Edinburgh: Handsel, 1981)

Cynthia Winton-Henry and Phil Porter, *Body and Soul: Excursions in the Realm of Physicality and Spirituality* (Oakland, CA: Wing It!, 1993)

Nicholas Wolterstorff, *Art in Action* (Grand Rapids: Eerdmans, 1980; re-issued Carlisle: Solway 1997)

Journals

Art and Christianity Enquiry
Tom Devonshire Jones ed., 4 Regents Park Road, London NW1 7TX, UK

Artyfact (quarterly) and *Articulate*
Journals from the Arts Centre Group focusing on support and encouragement for Christians in the arts, and in-depth articles on the interface between faith and art.
Anthony Nanson, ed. ACG, The Courtyard, 59a Portobello Road, London W11 3DB, UK
+44 (20) 7243 4550

Christianity and the Arts Magazine
Marci Whitney-Schenck, Publisher and Editor, P.O. Box 118088, Chicago,
   IL 60611, USA
   +1 (312) 642 8606.
   http: //www.christianarts.net/

Christianity and Theatre Magazine
(Bi-annual) PO Box 26471, Greenville, SC 29616 USA
   http: //www.cita.org

Cross Rhythms Magazine
PO Box 1110, Stoke-on-Trent, ST4 8JR, England
   http: //www.crossrhythms.co.uk/

Image: A Journal of the Arts and Religion
Gregory Wolfe ed., (Quarterly) PO Box 3000, Denville NJ07834; 323 S.
   Broad St., P.O. Box 674, Kennett Square, PA 19348, USA
   +1 (610) 925 4780
   http: //www.imagejournal.org

Third Way: The Modern World Through Christian Eyes
Huw Spanner ed., St Peter's, Sumner Road, Harrow, HA1 4BX, England
   +44 (20) 8423 8494

Worship Leader
Chuck Fromm ed. PO Box 408, Mt. Morris, IL, USA
   +1 (610) 548414
   http: //www.worshipleader.org/index.html

Useful Contacts

Actors Church Union
St. Paul's Church, Bedford Street, London WC2E 9ED, UK
+44 (20) 7836 5221
Serving the theatrical profession through members and 200 chaplains to theatres, studios and drama schools.

Artisan Initiative
Steve Cole (founder and director), PO Box 411, Shrewsbury SY3 8ST, UK
+44 (1743) 341 605
artisan.initiatives@dial.pipex.com
Artisan Initiatives was founded to create a sense of community and support base for people involved in Media and Entertainment through personal relationships, Backstage publication and prayer events. It also aims to inspire and educate the church in supporting these industries.

Arts Centre Group (ACG)
Steve Thomason (chair), The Courtyard, 59a Portobello Road, London W11 3DB, UK
+44 (20) 7243 4550
fax +44 (870) 706 0964
http://www.artscentregroup.org.uk
The ACG is a national association of Christian artists who seek to integrate their faith with their artistic activities. The ACG aims to unite and support Christian artists and performers from various disciplines so that they can be a transforming influence in the world of arts, media and entertainment.

Arts Council for Northern Ireland
181 Stranmillis Road, Belfast, BT9 5DU, UK
+44 (1232) 663591
http: //www.artscouncil-ni.org/
The principal channel for Government funding and development of the
contemporary arts in Northern Ireland. A source for advice and resources.

Arts Council of England
14 Great Peter Street, London, SW1P 3NQ, UK
+44 (20) 7 333 0100
http: //www.artscouncil.org.uk/
The principal channel for Government funding and development of the
contemporary arts in England. A source for advice and resources.

Arts Council of Wales
9 Museum Place, Cardiff, CF1 2NX, UK
+44 (1222) 376500
http: //www.ccc-acw.org.uk/
The principal channel for Government funding and development of the
contemporary arts in Wales. A source for advice and resources.

Art and Christianity Enquiry (ACE)
Tom Devonshire Jones (Director), 107 Crundale Avenue, London NW9 9PS,
UK
Tel / fax +44 (20) 8206 2253
A forum for those interested in the encounter between the arts (especially
the visual arts) and Christianity to share interests, projects and concerns. A
network as well as a pressure group seeking to improve training of clergy
and of church people in general, an organizer of events of specialist and
general interest and a resource centre.

Arts In Mission
Hermione Thompson, 4 Targetts Mead, Duck Street, Tisbury, Wiltshire
SP3 6SR, UK
+44 (1747) 870036
Elaine and David Chalmers-Brown, 24 Yorkshire Place, Warfield, Berkshire,
RG42 3XE, UK
+44 (1344) 426286
http: //www.wordnet.co.uk/arts.html
Aims to encourage, enable and equip Christians within the full spectrum of
the arts. To assist the whole church in mission and catalyze synergy between
the church and the arts.

Association of Christians in Planning & Architecture
38, De Montfort Street, Leicester LE1 7GP, UK
ACPA@uccf.org.uk
A support network.

Association of Christians in Local Broadcasting (ACLB)
PO Box 124, Westcliff on Sea, Essex SS0 0QU, UK
A support network.

Association of Christian Writers
Administrator: Warren Crawford, 73, Lodge Hill Road, Farnham, Surrey
GU10 3RB, UK
+44 (1252) 715 746
http://www.christianwriters.org.uk/
Aims to inspire and equip men and women to use their talents and skills
with integrity to devise, write and market excellent material which comes
from a Christian worldview.

Australian Christian Artists Network
ACAN – PO Box 2359 Rowville VIC 3178, Australia
+61 (3) 9795 7801
http://www.acan.org.au/
An Australian resource-based organization for Christian artists and those
wishing to find artists and groups for Christian arts projects.

Bible Society (BFBS)
Stonehill Green, Westlea, Swindon SN5 7DA, UK
+44 (1793) 418100
http://www.biblesociety.org.uk
Committed to finding fresh, innovative ways of re-telling God's story in
today's culture. Involvement in creative, imaginative and credible new
avenues in education, politics, media and the arts.

CHIME
Sarum College, 19 The Close, Salisbury, Wiltshire, SP1 2EE, UK
+44 (1722) 424805
fax +44 (1722) 338508
secretary@chime.org.uk
http://www.chime.org.uk
Aims to encourage good practice in the education and training of church
musicians.

Christian Copyright Licensing International
PO Box 1339, Eastbourne, E Sussex, BN21 4YF, UK
+44 (1323) 417 711
http: //www.ccli.com
A resource and advisory body regarding all issues of Christian copyright.
Christian Copyright Licensing Ltd

Christian Dance Fellowship of Britain
25 Scardale Crescent, Scarborough, N Yorks YO12 6LA, UK
+44 (1723) 377320
http: //www.cdfb.org.uk/
Seeks to support and encourage dance and creative movement as an expression
of the Christian faith.

Christian Drummers Association
c/o 15 Athlone Street, Tingalpa 4173, Australia
http: //www.powerup.com.au/~johnmoss/
Encourages Christian drummers of all levels to become involved in music
ministry by using their God-given gifts and skills.

Christian European Visual Media Association
c/o Box 1444, 35573 Wetzlar, Germany
+49 (6441) 957266
http: //www.webcom.com/nlnnet/cevma.html
An association of Christians who are involved in Visual Media – resources,
advice and networking

Christian Fellowship of Art Music Composers
Dr. Mark Hijleh (President), School of Music, Houghton College, Houghton,
NY 14744, USA
+1 (716) 567 9424
http: //www.cfamc.org
Encourages the work and witness of Christian composers of symphonic and
chamber music, opera and other serious concert works.

Christian Performing Artists' Fellowship (CPAF)
Patrick Kavanaugh (Executive Director), P.O. Box 800, Haymarket, Virginia
20168 USA
+1 (703) 753 0334
http: //www.christianperformingart.org
A classical music and dance ministry dedicated to performing to the glory
of God and to spreading the gospel of Jesus Christ. Now includes over
700 musicians and dancers.

Christians in Entertainment
Chris Gidney (Director), 54 The Glade, Old Coulsdon, Surrey CR5 1SL, UK
+1 (1737) 550375
http: //www.cieweb.org.uk
Promotes a Christian presence in the entertainment sector in Britain by providing support to professionals within the industry. It seeks to engage both Christians and those of little or no faith and aims to help the church to understand, support and pray for the entertainment business.

Christians in the Arts Networking
21 Harlow Street, PO Box 242, Arlington MA 02174 0003, USA
+1 (617) 646 1541
CANHep@uol.com
A global database for networking Christian artists, groups, festivals, conferences, colleges, etc.

Christians in Theatre Arts (CITA)
PO Box 26471, Greenville, SC 29616, USA
http: //www.cita.org
Seeks to 'impact the World and further the kingdom of God by encouraging and equipping Christians in the theatre arts.' It has a very comprehensive resource web site, runs conferences and publishes 'Christianity and Theatre' magazine.

Christians in the Visual Arts (CIVA)
Civa Membership, P.O. Box 18117, Minneapolis, MN 55418–0117, USA
+1 (508) 945 4026
http: //www.civa.org/
Explores and nurtures the relationship between the visual arts and the Christian faith.

Christian Writers Fellowship International (CWFI)
c/o Sandy Brooks, 1624 Jefferson Davis Rd., Clinton, SC 29325, USA
+1 (864) 697 6035
http: //www.cwfi-online.org/
A multi-service ministry for Christians in publishing. Encourages and equips writers to minister through writing of the highest biblical and professional standards.

The Churches' Advisory Council for Local Broadcasting
Jeff Bonser (General Secretary), Churches Advisory Council for Local Broadcasting, PO Box 124, Westcliff on Sea, Essex SS0 0QU, UK
+ 44 (1702) 348369
http: //www.caclb.org.uk/pages/caclb.html
Organization for the development, encouragement and promotion of Christian involvement in all aspects of local and regional broadcasting in the UK.

The Craft Council
44A Pentonville Road, London N1 9BY, UK
+44 (20) 7278 7700
http: //www.craftscouncil.org.uk/
The UK's national organization for the promotion of contemporary crafts. An independent body funded by the Arts Council of England, responsible for promoting fine craftsmanship, encouraging high standards and increasing public awareness of contemporary crafts and applied arts.

CTVC
The Foundation for Christian Communication Limited, Hillside, Merry Hill Road, Bushey, Herts WD2 1DR, UK
+44 (20) 8950 4426
http: //www.ctvc.co.uk
A British television production company specializing in programmes that focus on social, religious, educational and ethical issues in the broadcast sense. CTVC's productions include several series for BBC, ITV and Channel 4 as well as individual programmes.

Directory of Social Change
24 Stephenson Way, London NW1 2DP, UK
+44 (20) 7209 5151
http: //www.dsc.org.uk
Helps voluntary and community organizations become more effective by providing practical, challenging and affordable information and training to meet the current, emerging and future needs of the sector. Produces a wide range of publications to help charity fund raisers.

Epicentre
St. Marks Centre, Boutflower Road, Battersea, London SW11 4RE, UK
http: //web.ukonline.co.uk/epicentre
A group based in the Battersea/Clapham area of London which seeks to explore Christian spirituality in the context of the modern western world.

Fellowship of Artists in Cultural Evangelism (FACE)
605 E Elizabeth Street, Pasadena, CA 91104, USA
Trains, recruits, and mobilizes Christian artists to reach the unreached
peoples of the world in the context of their own cultures.

Fellowship of Christian Writers
76 Sarum Crescent, Wokingham, Berkshire RG40 1XF, UK

Fellowship of European Broadcasters
23, The Service Road, Potters Bar, Hertfordshire EN6 1QA, UK
http: //www.feb.org
Encourages co-operation and co-ordination between Christians in the
European Broadcasting Media. Provides a forum for the exchange of news,
to create opportunities for joint ventures and training. Represents the
interests of European Christians in the context of world broadcasting; to
encourage the highest professional and ethical standards; and to be a
credible voice to the European Community and to Governments.

Genesis Arts Trust
Nigel Goodwin (International Director), 6 Broad Court, London WC2B 5QZ,
UK
Promotes the Christian faith in the Arts and Media through the personal
ministry of Nigel Goodwin to numerous individuals in the world of arts and
entertainment.

Good News Music Society
GNMS Order Dept., 10415 Beardslee Blvd, Bothell, WA 98011–3271, USA
http: //www.gnms.com/
Source for church music, worship and drama resources, hymnals, robes,
folders, music gifts, etc.

Greenbelt
Andy Thornton (Festival Manager), The Greenhouse, Hillmarton Road,
London N7 9JE, UK
+44 (20) 7700 6585
http: \\www.greenbelt.org.uk
Greenbelt is an annual Christian arts festival that explores and celebrates
the Christian Gospel in relation to contemporary culture.

Institute of Leisure and Amenity Management (ILAM)
ILAM House, Lower Basildon, Reading, Berkshire RG8 9NE, UK
+44 (1491) 874800
http: //www.ilam.co.uk/
Represents every aspect of leisure, cultural and recreation management and is committed to the improvement of management standards through providing resources and other support.

L'Abri
The Manor House, Greatham, Near Liss, Hampshire GU33 6HF, UK
+44 (1420) 538436
http: //www.labri.org
Study centres in Europe, Asia and America where individuals have the opportunity to seek answers to honest questions about God and the significance of human life. L'Abri believes that Christianity speaks to all aspects of life.

Langham Arts Trust
St.Paul's Church, Robert Adam Street, London W1M 5AH, UK
+44 (20) 7935 7246
http: //www.andelscott.co.uk/aso/larts.htm
Promotes and supports the ministry of the famous All Souls Orchestra. A main aim is to promote events which seek to use music to glorify God, and provide an introduction for the non-Christian to the reality of the gospel.

Leith School of Art
25 North Junction Street, Edinburgh, Lothian EH6 6HW, UK
+44 (131) 554 5761
A visual arts school with a Christian foundation.

Media and Theology Project
New College, Edinburgh University, Mound Place, Edinburgh, EH1 2LX, UK
http: //www.div.ed.ac.uk/research/com/com.htm
An Edinburgh University project that aims to study the theological and ethical implications of communication and mass media.

Performing Rights Society Ltd.
29/33 Berners Street, London W1P 4AA, UK
+44 (20) 7580 5544
Deal with performing rights issues and legislation in the UK.

Reformation of the Arts and Music
http: //www.artsreformation.com
A web site with a large number of articles and resources. Seeks 'to encourage appreciation of the arts, thereby improving the quality of the arts, so that the arts may develop richly and abundantly, bestowing its wealth upon the whole of society, in accordance with the Christian worldview, leading to a Reformation of the Arts and Music.'

Riding Lights Theatre Company
Friargate Theatre, Lower Friargate, York YO1 9SL, UK
http: //www.ridinglights.org
The most well-known and well-established UK Christian theatre company with advice and resources galore.

School of Creative Ministries
Kensington Temple, Kensington Park Road, London W11 3BY, UK
+44 (20) 7727 4877
http: //www.ken-temp.org.uk/ibiol/scm.htm
A performing arts course at the International Bible Institute of London at which Christians can explore and develop their creative abilities in a Christian environment.

Seeds
24, Meadway Close, New Barnet, Herts EN5 5 LA, UK
+44 (20) 8364 9652
Scottish Arts Council
19 Charlotte Square, Edinburgh, EH2 4DF, UK
+44 (131) 226 6051
http: //www.sac.org.uk
The principal channel for Government funding and development of the contemporary arts in Scotland. A source for advice and resources.

Theology Through the Arts
Ridley Hall, Cambridge, CB3 9HG, UK
+44 (1223) 741072
http: //www.theolarts.org
A project based in Cambridge and St Andrews that aims to discover and demonstrate ways in which the arts can contribute to a renewal of Christian theology.

Universities and Colleges Christian Fellowship (UCCF)
38, De Monfort Street, Leicester LE1 7GP, UK
+44 (116) 255 1700
http: //www.uccf.org.uk
An organization with advice and resources on all things Christian.
Worship Resource Center
http: //praise.net/worship
A useful web site for arts in worship resources.

UK Christian Handbook
Christian Research Association, Vision Building, 4 Footscray Road,
Eltham, London SE9 2TZ, UK
http: //www.ukchristianhandbook.org.uk/
UK Christian resource directory.